Also by the Author

Manhattan

The Erin O'Reilly Mysteries
Book Five

Steven Henry

Clickworks Press • Baltimore, MD

First publication: Clickworks Press, 2019
Release: CP-EOR5-INT-P.IS-1.0

Sign up for updates, deals, and exclusive sneak peeks at clickworkspress.com/join.

ISBN-13: 978-1-943383-49-8
ISBN-10: 1-943383-49-9

For the first responders, the ones who run toward the gunshots and into the fire.

Manhattan

Combine 1 oz. rye whiskey, .5 oz. sweet vermouth, and 3 dashes of aromatic bitters in a jigger. Stir and strain into a cocktail glass. Garnish with a cherry and serve.

Chapter 1

Erin O'Reilly walked into the Barley Corner with Rolf, her partner, at her side. The pub was full of the usual patrons, mostly male, mostly Irish. It was just after work, so the majority were still sober. She made her way toward the bar, threading through the crowd. A lot of women would've felt uncomfortable in that setting. She knew she was attractive, and she kept up her athletic figure with an early-morning run every day. But the regulars at the Corner knew Erin, and while several pairs of eyes followed her appreciatively, no one said anything or stepped out of line. They knew she was off-limits.

That was because Erin was a cop, a detective with the Major Crimes Division. And there was Erin's partner to consider. Rolf was ninety pounds of highly-trained German Shepherd K-9. Plus, she was tight with the Corner's proprietor, Morton "Cars" Carlyle, and nobody wanted to be on his bad side. Carlyle was a wiseguy, middle management in the O'Malley branch of the Irish Mob.

She nodded a greeting to the bartender as she slipped onto a stool. "Evening, Danny." Rolf sat beside the barstool and watched the room.

"Evening, Erin," Danny said, grinning cheerfully. "You on the clock?"

"Just punched out."

"Usual, then?"

"Sure thing."

Danny slid a shot of Glen D whiskey across the bar to her. He didn't ask for payment. Erin had saved Carlyle's life three months earlier when hitmen had shown up gunning for him. Before that, she'd helped disarm a bomb practically out of Danny's own hands. As long as the Corner was under Carlyle's management, Erin drank on the house.

She'd become a regular at the Corner. It was the closest bar to her apartment, a few minutes' easy walk, and it was a classy joint, in spite of the clientele. Or maybe because of them. Carlyle kept his place in order.

The strangest thing about Erin's life these days was her growing relationship with Carlyle. Even a kid could tell they were natural enemies. What preschooler didn't know how to play cops and robbers? But fate had lined them up on the same side more than once. Erin had protected Carlyle's business, and his life, and in return he'd helped her close a couple of cases. In the process, they'd come to understand one another. They lived in the same world and knew its rules better than any outsider. There were things she couldn't ask him, and things he couldn't tell her, but as long as they stayed off those subjects, they got along great.

As if she'd called him, there he was at her elbow, a handsome, silver-haired Irishman, a few years older than she, impeccably dressed in a charcoal gray suit and matching tie. "Evening, darling," he said. "I hope Danny's taking good care of you?"

"Always," she said with a smile. "How's business?"

"Oh, grand. God pours souls into Irishmen, a publican pours

spirits into them."

She laughed. "You're just lucky they don't bring back Prohibition."

"Are you serious? I'd see my profits grow tenfold if the government ever did such a foolish thing."

"You're probably right," she admitted. "My dad said that turned more cops dirty than anything else in New York history." Erin's dad had been a Patrol officer with the NYPD.

Both of them recognized they were skating close to dangerous ground. Carlyle changed the subject.

"You strike me as rather cheerful compared to the end of your typical workday. Did you close a significant case?"

"It's actually been pretty quiet," she said ruefully.

"Surely a lack of serious crime is something your lads ought to celebrate."

Erin laughed again. "Mostly we just get bored and bitch at each other. This is more of a personal thing."

He raised an eyebrow. "Ought I to order a drink of my own?"

"Depends. I just got some good news."

"Then I'll surely share a drink with you," Carlyle said. He raised a finger to Danny, and a drink appeared in front of him. "Don't keep me in suspense."

"Remember the serial killer thing a couple months back?"

"Aye."

"Captain Holliday was impressed," she said. "They're bumping me up to Detective Second Grade, effective at the start of next week."

"Ah, Erin, that's grand news!" Carlyle exclaimed. He clinked his glass against hers. "You've not been a detective long. I'm glad to see they're already aware of your quality."

She'd been surprised by the news herself. The captain had called her into his office at the end of the shift, given her a brisk handshake and a nod, and said, "Good work, Detective. Keep it up." For Holliday, that counted as a strong display of emotion.

"At this rate, you'll be Commissioner of Police by the time you're forty," Carlyle went on.

"I'd rather have my fingernails pulled," she said, grimacing. "Without anesthetic."

"Always the woman of action," he said with a twinkle in his eye. "Never the bureaucrat."

"If I'd wanted a desk job, there's plenty out there."

Carlyle glanced away for a moment, catching movement near the door. Erin followed his look and saw a slender, red-haired man threading the crowd toward them. She recognized him immediately; James Corcoran, Carlyle's best friend. He'd been trying to charm Erin into bed since the moment they'd met, and had nearly succeeded before she'd found out that, in addition to being witty, friendly, and sexy as hell, he was a notorious smuggler, sometime knife-fighter, and another member of the O'Malleys. Corky had taken Erin's brushoff as nothing but a temporary setback at first and continued flirting with her whenever they met. He'd backed off a little, but Erin wasn't sure he'd given up hope.

"Oh God," she said, but she smiled as she said it. It was hard not to like Corky.

"He'll be pleased to drink to your news, I'll warrant," Carlyle said.

"He'll drink to anything," she retorted. "He'd drink to the end of the world."

"And say it wasn't a moment too soon," Carlyle agreed. He shifted his attention to Corky and his welcoming smile faded. "What's up?" he said more sharply.

Corky's usual boyish grin was nowhere in sight. His green eyes were as cold and serious as Erin had ever seen, and that included the time she'd stood next to him while he held a live explosive device. "We need to talk," he said, ignoring Erin completely. That was unprecedented. As long as Corky had a pulse, he noticed attractive women.

"I suppose we do," Carlyle said. Always the gentleman, he turned to Erin. "Will you please excuse us?"

She nodded. "Sure." But she was worried. From the look of them, some serious shit had just gone down in their world. And in their world, bad news usually meant bodies.

The two Irishmen left the bar and went quickly to the back of the room, through the door that led to Carlyle's private upstairs suite. Erin watched them go, wanting to follow them, to ask questions, but knowing she'd get no answers. She wondered whether she'd find out from the other side, when the fallout from their troubles crossed her own desk.

"Get you anything else?" Danny asked on his way from one end of the bar to the other. Erin looked down and saw that her glass was empty. She also saw that Carlyle hadn't finished his own drink, nor taken it with him. This was serious, all right.

"No thanks," she said.

Her phone buzzed in her pocket. She started, then fished it out, feeling a little silly for her nerves. She saw the name of her commanding officer on her caller ID and sighed. Lieutenant Webb didn't make courtesy calls. This was business.

She thumbed her screen. "O'Reilly."

"Where are you?" Webb asked. No small talk, straight to the point.

"At a bar."

"Not drunk, are you?"

"No, sir. Just had one."

"Okay, get back here right now."

"Sure thing." She pushed back from the bar and hopped off the stool. Rolf followed. "What've we got?"

"A 10-13 just came over the net."

Erin didn't understand. The code for an officer needing assistance was important, sure, but they wouldn't rope in an off-duty detective for it. There were literally thousands of officers already on duty who could respond more quickly. "I'll get there as quick as I can, but—"

He cut her off. "It's too late for that. We got an officer down."

Her heart lurched. "We have units on scene?"

"Yeah," Webb said. But she already knew from his tone what he was going to say. "We lost him."

She didn't want to ask the next question, but she had to know. "Who is it?"

Webb hesitated a second too long. Names chased each other through her brain. She felt like she was going to throw up.

"He's one of ours," he said. "From the Eightball. It's Hendricks, a rookie. Bob Michaelson's partner."

Erin had to stop moving for a second and close her eyes. She knew Michaelson. "What happened?"

"We're detectives, O'Reilly. It's our job to find that out."

Chapter 2

The scene of the shooting was just off FDR Drive, near the East River. A full squadron of NYPD cruisers had deployed on Fletcher Street, under FDR. Grim-faced uniformed officers were everywhere. Erin even saw half a dozen guys in full ESU tactical gear, assault rifles in their hands.

The other members of Erin's squad were already there. Vic Neshenko gave her a curt nod. Kira Jones looked at Erin with haunted eyes.

"Hey, Erin," Kira said quietly.

"Hey," Erin replied, unable to think of anything else to say.

"I heard they pushed you up to Second Grade," Vic said to Erin by way of greeting.

"Yeah." She hadn't wanted to bring it up. Vic was still a Detective Third Grade, and had been wearing a gold shield longer than her. She wasn't sure how he felt about her being bumped past him.

"I suppose that means you're gonna be looking for more respect," he said.

"No, I expect you'll still be an asshole."

"Okay. No problem, then."

If Vic ever went to prison, he'd never get time off for good behavior, but Erin liked him. However surly he got, he was rock solid when things went sideways. There was no man in the NYPD she'd prefer to have watching her back.

"How long had Hendricks been wearing his shield?" she wondered aloud.

"The hell would I know? I guess maybe he was with the last Academy class."

"Jesus," Erin said. "On the Job less than a year."

"It's always the newbies that get it," he said. "They can't read the street yet."

"That's why they have training officers," she said.

"Yeah," Vic said. "What the hell was Michaelson doing, letting this happen? He's been around longer than God. Never lost another partner."

"I'll bet Michaelson's asking himself the same thing," Erin said. She was thinking of John Brunanski, the officer who'd died holding her hand. She still thought about what she could've, should've done differently, all the ways she could've saved him.

"Hell of a thing," Vic said.

"Yeah."

"Okay, team," Webb said. "We're all thinking it. This is a shitty situation. But every case we get is shit. They don't call Major Crimes over parking tickets. Let's work the case and get it solved."

The crime scene was obvious. A squad car was angled across the narrow street, both front doors standing open. The detectives gathered around the car and stared. The passenger-side window was a maze of cracked safety glass. It had three bullet holes, tightly grouped. Blood was spattered on the door panel and pooled on the pavement. Discarded bits of packaging for first-aid supplies were strewn around. There was no body.

"Where's Hendricks?" Webb asked the nearest uniform.

"I heard they took him to Bellevue," the officer replied.

"Small world," Erin muttered. Her oldest brother was a trauma surgeon there.

"What's that, Detective?" the patrolman asked.

"Never mind," she said.

Bob Michaelson was sitting on the curb a little ways off. He was a heavyset Patrol sergeant in his mid-forties. Today, he looked twice that old. The other officers had given Michaelson some respectful space, so he sat all alone. He was covered with blood. Hands, face, uniform. Someone had put a paper cup of coffee in his hand. He didn't seem to have noticed it.

"Poor guy," Kira said softly.

Webb sighed. "Let's get this over with." They walked to stand in front of Michaelson. He didn't look up.

Webb cleared his throat. "Excuse me, Sergeant."

Michaelson raised his head. He looked straight through Webb.

"What happened, Bob?" Webb asked, his voice surprisingly gentle.

"Normal patrol," Michaelson said. He sounded hoarse, like a man who'd smoked too many cigarettes. "Same shit, different day. We came down Maiden Lane. I saw that door," he waved a hand indifferently toward the building behind him, "and spotted a possible forced entry."

Erin looked over Michaelson's shoulder. Sure enough, the warehouse at his back had a door that was standing ajar. She could see splintered wood on the doorframe, probably from a crowbar.

"Tim called it in," Michaelson went on. "I parked across Fletcher. Just then, the break-in crew came out."

"Carrying anything?" Webb asked.

"Duffel bags," Michaelson said. "Three suspects. Tim wanted to bust them right there, but I got an ID on their leader.

I told Tim to call for backup, to fall back. But the kid wanted the collar. You know how rookies are. He was out of the car before I could stop him. He didn't listen." The old sergeant put a hand over his face. "I told him to get back in the car. He didn't listen."

"Bob," Webb said, "you know who the shooter was?"

He nodded. "I got a great look at his face. But it happened so goddamn *fast*. Bastard had his gun out the second Tim yelled 'NYPD!' I was still getting out my side of the car. The son of a bitch put three through the window there. Tim didn't even get a shot off, caught two right in the throat."

"Holy shit," Vic said softly. He was looking at the car door, tracing bullet trajectories with his fingertip. "That's some damn good shooting."

"Bob," Webb said again, "who the hell did this?"

Michaelson finally met Webb's eye. "Hans Rüdel."

*   *   *

"No."

Erin and Vic said it simultaneously. They glanced at one another, then back at Michaelson.

"That's not possible," Erin said.

"Rüdel's dead," Vic said. "That's not rumor, it's a goddamn fact. I put two bullets in his chest. I watched him go into the East River."

"I was there," Erin said. "I saw it too."

"Then he's got a twin brother," Michaelson said. "Because I just watched him mow down my partner."

"You're sure it was him?" Erin pressed.

"He was ten yards away, tops. His face was all over the news this summer. Yeah, I'm sure."

Corky and Carlyle's behavior suddenly made sense to Erin. Rüdel had tried to kill Carlyle and nearly succeeded. If Corky had heard he was back in circulation, the Irishmen had a very big problem.

Vic abruptly walked away from the damaged squad car. He went around the corner of the warehouse and out of sight. Webb and Kira were still talking to Michaelson, but Erin didn't think they'd find out much more. She and Rolf went after Vic.

She rounded the corner just in time to see the big Russian slam his hand against the brickwork. He pulled back his arm and did it again, then a third time. As she came cautiously toward him, he clenched his fists and let out one word.

"Fuck!"

Erin put out a hand and touched his shoulder. "Vic," she said. "Breathe, big guy."

He leaned against the wall with both hands, letting his head hang down between his shoulders. "I missed," he said.

"No you didn't," she said. "I was there. You nailed him twice."

"Should've made it three. Should've put one in his damn face. He was right there, he was wounded, we had him! We were so goddamn sure he was dead, we didn't look hard enough. And now that kid's dead. Because of me."

"Knock it off!" Erin snapped. "You are so full of shit. Hendricks is dead because we've got the most dangerous job in New York. He got careless and eager. You didn't make him get out of that car. You're blaming yourself, Michaelson's blaming himself, the only reason Hendricks isn't blaming himself is that he's not alive to do it. Rüdel's the only one to blame. Will you lay off the self-pity so we can get some work done?"

Vic looked at her, and she was ashamed of herself when she saw the raw pain in his eyes. But it was only for a second. Then he locked it away in some deep, dark part of himself. He blinked, and when he opened his eyes, his game face was on.

"You can be a cold, hard bitch, you know that?" he said.

"Had a lot of punks tell me that over the years," she replied.

"You know I love you for it."

"You getting mushy on me now?"

His lips moved in a grim parody of a smile. "Okay, tell me one thing. Get it right, and maybe I really will kiss you. How the hell do we find this bastard?"

Erin hadn't been thinking of much else. "First we need his motive."

"That's easy. He didn't want to go to prison."

"No, not why he shot Hendricks. I mean, why was he breaking into this building in the first place?"

Vic thumped the bricks and winced.

"You okay?" Erin asked.

He studied his hand. Lines of blood streaked his palm. "Yeah, I'm fine."

"Better put on some gloves before we check the scene," she said. "Let's find out what Rüdel stole."

*　　*　　*

They couldn't just go inside. The Fourth Amendment, and the Supreme Court, dictated that the police needed a warrant unless they could show imminent danger to life or risk of destruction of evidence. Neither of those stipulations applied in this case, so they had to jump through the bureaucratic hoops. The silly thing was, everyone knew they'd get the warrant, but they still couldn't go in until they had it. Sillier still, they couldn't contact the owner of the warehouse.

"The lease is under the name Jameson," Kira said after some quick digging through a squad-car computer. "As in, the whiskey. But I think it's a front. There's a phone number, but it goes to generic voicemail."

"We don't need the owner's permission," Webb said. "But it

sounds like they're into something shady."

"Surprise," Vic muttered. "What, did you think he was stealing jelly beans?"

"Got the warrant," Kira announced.

"Okay," Webb said. "It's unlikely any of Rüdel's guys are still inside, but let's exercise some caution. Guns out, people."

They roped in a couple of ESU operators, just in case. The tactical guys lined up with the detectives outside. Webb cleared his throat.

"This is the NYPD! We're coming in to execute a search warrant. Anyone in there, keep your hands where we can see them!"

Vic and one of the ESU went first. Erin, Rolf, and another ESU guy followed. Webb and Kira brought up the rear with a small posse of NYPD uniforms. They moved quickly to clear the kill-zone in the doorway. The door itself was already broken and posed no obstacle.

Erin was tense and keyed up, ready for anything. She reminded herself to check her corners, to keep her field of fire clear. She could feel the nervous energy in her fellow officers. They were looking for some payback for Hendricks.

Vic was a big guy, and so was the ESU man beside him. All Erin could really see to her front was their shoulders and the backs of their heads and vests. When they suddenly stopped, just a few feet inside, she nearly ran into Vic.

"Freeze!" Vic shouted. "Hands up!"

There was a momentary pause. Erin sidestepped, keeping partially behind Vic's bulk. She brought her Glock in line and peered around him. Then she saw that she hadn't really been ready for anything.

A gorgeous redhead sitting calmly on a packing crate hadn't entered into her predictions for how this search was likely to go.

The woman looked to be in her mid to late twenties. She

was dressed in dark, tight jeans and a black leather jacket that was open in front. Under it was a form-fitting black turtleneck showing off a fantastic figure. Her long, wavy hair was coppery auburn, pulled back in a ponytail that made her look younger than she probably was. Her face was oval-shaped with high cheekbones. Her eyes were bright, penetrating green.

The woman slowly showed her hands to the police. She stood up, unhurried, ignoring the guns pointed her way. Then she smiled.

Erin saw something predatory in the expression. It was a fierce look. A hint of teeth showed between the lips.

The red-haired woman said, "Easy on those triggers, lads. You wouldn't want to be doing something we'd all regret, would you?"

Erin started at the unmistakable brogue of Northern Ireland. The woman could've come from the same neighborhood as Corky and Carlyle from the sound of her.

"What's your name, ma'am?" Vic demanded. He was still aiming his Sig-Sauer at her and seemed totally unimpressed with her feminine charms.

"Siobhan Finneran, lad," she said. "You're a bit tight-wound, aren't you? What do you call yourself, big fellow?"

"Detective Neshenko," Vic said. He, Erin, and one of the ESU guys moved in on her while the rest of the police spread out to finish clearing the warehouse.

"I'm Detective O'Reilly," Erin added.

Siobhan turned her attention to Erin, who caught a flicker of surprise in her eyes. Surprise, and maybe even recognition. Erin tried to remember whether she'd met Siobhan before. She was sure she wouldn't have forgotten someone so striking.

"O'Reilly?" Siobhan said sardonically. "Another Irishwoman. Oh, that's grand."

"Are you carrying any weapons, Ms. Finneran?" Vic asked.

"That depends on one's definition."

"Guns, knives, sharp objects," he said, refusing to flirt.

"Nay, nothing of that sort."

"We need to check you anyway," he said. "Erin can do it if you're not comfortable with a man—"

"You needn't worry about my tender feelings," she said. "Or are you doubting your self-control?"

"I'll do it," Erin said to preempt whatever retort Vic was brewing up. "Please extend your arms to either side, ma'am."

"Ma'am," Siobhan snorted. "You're years older, I'm thinking." She obeyed, but as Erin began patting her down, she looked the policewoman over. Erin felt like the search was a mutual thing. She didn't like the feeling.

"You're not as pretty as I thought," Siobhan said in a quieter tone.

"Do I know you?" Erin asked.

"Oh no, ma'am. I'd remember."

Erin ran her hands over the other woman's shoulders and down her sides, repeating the basic frisking procedure she'd done dozens of times on patrol. Then she felt something and stopped. There was definitely a bulge under Siobhan's left arm.

"Ms. Finneran," Erin said, speaking with deliberate slowness, not wanting to startle anyone into rash action. "What have you got under your jacket?"

"It's a holster," Siobhan said.

"Whoa there," Vic said. "You said you weren't armed!"

"I'm not," she said. "It's simply a holster, no revolver in it. Feel free to check."

Erin wasn't about to take the woman at her word. She flipped back the leather jacket and saw it was true. Siobhan was wearing a shoulder holster, but it was empty.

"Where's the gun?" Erin asked.

"What gun?"

"Your gun."

"You can see I've no gun on my person. I'm breaking no laws."

We'll see about that, Erin thought and almost said out loud. What she did say was, "We're still going to need you to come with us and answer some more questions."

"Am I under arrest?"

"Only if you refuse."

Siobhan smiled icily. "An Irishwoman doesn't make idle threats."

Erin gave a cold smile of her own. "If I threaten you, Ms. Finneran, you'll know it."

They glared at each other for a long moment. Erin knew the other woman didn't like her, and that it was something that went beyond her being a cop, but she didn't understand what it could be. Maybe she'd arrested Siobhan's brother, or lover, or something. Whatever it was, Siobhan was giving her the sort of look that on the street usually meant a fight would to be on in a few seconds.

Kira saw it too. She interposed herself between the two women. "I'll escort Ms. Finneran to the precinct," she said. "Why don't you and Rolf case the scene, make sure we don't miss anything?"

"Right," Erin said. As she turned away, she paused. "Make sure you check her for powder residue."

"Will do," Kira said.

"Oh aye, that's exactly the sort of thing a lass might do," Siobhan said. "Engage in a bit of pistol-play, then simply hang about the place waiting for the coppers. If I had bloody rocks in my head, maybe that's what I'd have done, but perhaps I'd simply have joined your police department instead."

Erin let the cheap shot pass. "Rolf," she said to her K-9, "*such.*"

It was his search command, spoken in his native German. The Shepherd put his nose to the ground and started sniffing. He was trained to search for humans, both living and dead, and explosives. She'd know what he found by his reaction. He scratched and whined when he located a person. If he smelled a bomb, he sat perfectly still and stared at it. Trainers had learned long ago that a dog pawing at an explosive device wasn't the best idea.

"We're clear," one of the ESU guys announced. The warehouse was half-full of packing crates and forklift palettes. There was a small office with an adjoining restroom, along with a maintenance room and a couple of empty side rooms. The police had checked all of these and found them vacant.

Erin wasn't expecting Rolf to find anything, but the Shepherd proved her wrong. He pulled toward the middle of one of the rows of boxes, then abruptly stopped and sat.

She took a look. Two big packing crates had been smashed open, probably with the same crowbar that had been used on the door. Their contents were jumbled, as if someone had rifled them in a quick search. It looked like they contained wool blankets.

"What've you got?" Vic asked, coming up behind her.

Erin had gone very cold inside. "I think he found what Rüdel was after," she said.

"What's that?"

She hoped like hell she was wrong. "A bomb was here."

Chapter 3

They didn't find much else in the warehouse. Specifically, they didn't find a gun belonging to Siobhan. If the woman had been armed when she'd come into the building, she'd hidden the weapon very well. Rolf didn't alert to any unopened boxes, and there weren't any explosives left behind in the open crates, so Rüdel had found everything of that sort there was to find.

And he'd known exactly where to look. No other boxes were disturbed. That fit his MO. The last time he'd gone looking for smuggled weapons, he'd tortured information out of the escort. Erin wondered how he'd come up with the info this time around.

They left the scene to the CSU guys and headed to the precinct. It was already dark by the time the forensic team arrived. Erin wished this hadn't happened at the end of a long workday.

"I know guys who'd kill for the overtime we pull," Kira said.

"I know guys who kill for all sorts of reasons," Vic said. "Working homicide cases lets you get to know people like that."

"Ha ha," Kira said. "You know what this kind of thing does to my love life?"

"No," Vic said, "but feel free to tell us. You can use pictures if you want."

"Picture this," Kira said, showing him an expressive single digit.

"Okay," Webb said, walking to the whiteboard in the middle of the Major Crimes headquarters. "We've got a known multiple murderer out there." He wrote Rüdel's name on top of the board. "Neshenko, pull this dirtbag's file. While you're at it, upgrade his status from 'presumed deceased' to 'pain in the ass.'"

"Got it," Vic said. He flopped down at his desk, opened a bottle of Mountain Dew, and got to work.

"Jones," Webb said. "How's our guest settling in?"

"I've got her in Interrogation Room One," Kira said. "No residue on her. If she was in the fight, she didn't fire, and she wasn't standing near anyone who did."

Webb sighed. "So what was she doing there?"

"She's dirty," Erin said. "Let me take a crack at her."

"You want her, you got her," Webb said. "You think it'll help or hurt having a guy in the room with you?"

"I got this," Erin said.

"Take Jones with you," he suggested. "I'll observe."

"Oh goody," Kira said. "Girls' night."

* * *

The chairs in the interrogation room were empty. Siobhan was leaning against the back wall, one knee bent, her foot pressed against the wall. Her hands were in her pockets. She smiled humorlessly at the two detectives.

"Why don't you sit down, Ms. Finneran, and we can talk," Kira suggested.

"I'm fine here," Siobhan replied.

"Have a seat," Erin said, phrasing it more like an order than a suggestion.

"And if I don't? Will you have that big lad of yours come in here and hold me down? He might enjoy it."

Kira sat in one of the chairs on their side of the table. Erin compromised and rested one hip on the table edge.

"Okay, Ms. Finneran," Erin said. "What were you doing in that warehouse?"

"My job."

"What's your job?"

"Inspection of merchandise."

"Who do you work for?"

"A shipping concern."

"What's it called?"

"You've my work visa," Siobhan said. That was true. They'd gotten her identification papers out of her wallet when they frisked her; she wasn't the sort of woman who carried a purse. Her ID claimed she was a native of Northern Ireland, born in Belfast. Her work visa identified her as a shipping manager for a company called Connaught Imports. Besides that, she had some cash and a cell phone on her person. The phone was a cheap flip-phone, and they didn't have a warrant for the call history.

"You're from Belfast," Erin said.

"You know how to read," Siobhan said. "I'm surprised they've not made you chief of the department."

"Have you been to New York before?"

"It's hard to say," Siobhan said. "I dreamed one night I died and went to heaven, but to an Irishwoman, heaven and New York are about the same. The promised land it is, sure enough, where our fathers and mothers are waiting for us."

"What sort of gun do you own?" Erin asked. She was deliberately jumping around different topics, trying to throw the other woman off-balance.

"I'd a water pistol when I was a wee lass," Siobhan said. "I used to fire it at potted plants about the neighborhood."

"How long have you been working for the O'Malleys?" It was a guess, but Erin thought it was a good one. Rüdel had been entangled with the Irish gang ever since he'd come to town.

"I work for Connaught Imports," Siobhan said. "I've worked for them since I was nineteen. How long have you been a copper?"

"Long enough to know what bullshit smells like," Erin said.

"Would that be your perfume of choice, then?" Siobhan inquired with false innocence.

"Why are you here?" Erin demanded, getting off the table and standing face-to-face with Siobhan.

"You brought me here."

Erin shook her head. "You know damn well what I mean."

"Then it's you who's doing a poor job of explaining yourself."

Kira quietly said, "I've been in the room with dozens of suspects."

The other two women both paused and looked at her.

"They tell all sorts of stories," Kira went on. "But one thing they've got in common is that the innocent ones don't evade. You're dancing and dodging around, and you probably think you're being clever, but all you're doing is looking guiltier and guiltier."

"Of what crime, precisely, are you accusing me?" Siobhan asked.

"Trafficking weapons," Erin said.

"Ah," Siobhan said. "And here I am with all these weapons about me. Whatever was I thinking?"

The Irishwoman's style of talking, the way she danced and dodged, as Kira had put it, reminded Erin of somebody else she knew, an Irishman with a talent for not answering questions.

Siobhan and Carlyle both hailed from Belfast. It was quite a coincidence, and eleven years of police work had taught Erin to be very suspicious of coincidences.

But this was getting them nowhere. Siobhan was too cagey. Besides, she actually hadn't done anything that they knew about or could prove. "We can hold you for twenty-four hours without charging you," Erin said.

"Is that intended to frighten me?" Siobhan shot back.

"Not really," Erin said. "I just figured you're here to do some work, and while you're in here, it's not getting done. I thought that might bother you."

Siobhan smiled coldly. "Then I'll just have to make up for lost time once I get out, won't I?"

* * *

"Well, that was interesting," Webb said. They were in the observation room, watching Siobhan through the one-way mirror. The Irishwoman was studying the fingernails on one hand with apparent unconcern.

"That's one word for it," Kira said. "That woman's up to something."

"Right," Webb said. He rubbed his forehead. "I'll talk to Judge Ferris, make sure that we can charge her with two or three felony counts of Being Up to Something. Then we're home free."

"Not even crazy old Ferris will sign out that warrant," Erin said. Ferris was years past retirement age, but still a good friend to law enforcement—when he was awake.

"We're wasting time on her," Vic said. "We should be out there chasing Rüdel down."

"She might know something about him," Erin said.

"Doesn't matter if she does," he said. "She's not gonna give us shit. We need leverage."

"Or more information," Erin said thoughtfully.

"I'm gonna be on the phone to Interpol again, aren't I," Vic said. "Shit. You know how hard it is to get through to those guys?"

"Yeah," Webb said. "But we need you to do it. If Finneran has priors, they'll probably be in Ireland."

"I'd better talk to my Irish contacts," Erin said. "Find out if anyone knows her."

"Be careful," Kira said. "Remember, Rüdel's been working for one of the O'Malleys. If you talk to one of his friends, you might get in trouble."

"I don't think that's gonna be a problem," Erin said.

Chapter 4

"Erin, darling," Carlyle said. "I wasn't expecting you to be returning this very evening."

By the time she'd gotten to the Corner it was after ten. The pub was packed with patrons. Carlyle was in his usual place. Whatever news Corky had brought, Carlyle seemed to have recovered. He didn't act any different than normal.

"Everything okay, Carlyle?" she asked, glancing around.

"Why wouldn't it be?"

"Corky. He wasn't himself earlier."

"Well, he is an emotional lad," Carlyle said. "Wears his heart on his sleeve."

"I don't see him here now."

"He'd some pressing business to attend to."

She leaned on the bar next to Carlyle and signaled Danny. "Gimme a Glen D, straight up," she said.

"Coming right up," he replied, grabbing a glass and pouring the whiskey.

"So, you're not working," Carlyle said.

"I need a damn drink," she said.

"Are we drinking to anything?"

She stared into the glass. "One of ours got killed tonight."

"A copper?"

"Yeah."

"Did you know him?"

"Not really," she said. "I saw him around the station a few times. He was a rookie. Did something dumb, got himself shot."

"I'm sorry to hear it," Carlyle said. He raised a finger to the bartender. "One for me, Danny. Same as she's having."

"It's crazy, you know," Erin said. She waited until Carlyle had a drink in front of him before taking a slug of her whiskey.

"What is?" he asked, matching her with a sip of his own.

"Drinking to the memory of a downed officer with a mob lieutenant."

"If it'll make you feel better, you can drink with me the next time one of my associates meets an untimely end."

"I think that'd just make it crazier," she said with a rueful laugh.

"Probably," he allowed. "But I am sorry this happened."

"That's the craziest thing of all," she said, meeting his eyes. "I actually believe you."

He smiled a surprisingly gentle smile. "Thank you. Do you want to talk about it?"

"No." She threw back the rest of her drink, embracing the burn in her throat. "I want to catch the son of a bitch who did it."

"I wish you the best of luck, then," Carlyle said. "I'm against the killing of coppers. At least," he amended, "American coppers. I never was overly fond of the Royal Ulster Constabulary."

Erin saw her opening. "What was it like, living in Northern Ireland?" she asked.

"What sort of a question is that, Erin? You wanting my whole life's story tonight?"

"No," she said. "I was just wondering how it felt, growing up in a place where you didn't trust the police, where they were the enemy."

"You could ask the inhabitants of one of your inner-city neighborhoods here. I imagine they'd tell you."

"That's a low blow."

"My apologies," he said. "I was merely observing there's a few similarities between America and Ireland."

"Okay, okay," she said. "But seriously. Tell me something about yourself. I've been wondering a few things."

He raised his eyebrows. "Ask away."

"You told me once about your wife."

A look of far-off sadness drifted into Carlyle's eyes. "Aye, Rosie."

"Was there ever another girl, over there? In Ireland, I mean?"

Carlyle finished his own drink and set the glass down firmly on the countertop. The sorrow was gone from his face. His eyes went hard and he met her stare without flinching. "I loved her," he said. "I was never unfaithful to her. Not once."

"That wasn't what I meant," Erin said, feeling herself flush. "Before you met her, or maybe after she died."

"Erin," he said, "why are you asking me this?"

"I'm just trying to figure you out."

"Are we exchanging stories here? Am I allowed to ask you similar sorts of things?"

"If you want."

"Very well," he said, pivoting on his stool so his back was to the bar and resting one arm along the hardwood. "Though Corky's a better lad to be talking to if you're wanting tales of romantic conquest. That lad cut a wide swath and left a trail of broken hearts behind him."

"He still does, I imagine," she said, smiling. "But I figure you're more likely to tell me something true."

Carlyle laughed.

"There's gotta be some girl you knew back in the day," Erin went on. "Hot young redhead, maybe?"

"Rosie was a brunette. And she wasn't what you'd call a bombshell. She'd a sweet face, the loveliest, kindest eyes you've ever seen. She was a farm lass from County Down, spent a lot of time out of doors, so she'd a sprinkling of freckles on her cheeks and nose. Rosie was always ashamed of them, but I thought they added something to her face. Nay, I wasn't one to go chasing the knockouts."

"Wow," Erin said.

"What?"

"You really are a romantic at heart."

He laughed again, quietly. "I suppose perhaps I am. Now, I've told you something about my true love. Tell me something about yours. That's only fair."

"I would if I could," she said. "I never had one."

"Never been in love?"

She shrugged. "Just teenage crushes. It's hard enough to meet guys under normal circumstances. The work I do, the hours I put in, it's not like I've got men lined up around the block. Plus, lots of them are intimidated by me. Can't think why, what with the gun, the shield, and the badass dog."

"I can see how that could be a difficulty," Carlyle said. "But I think you're selling yourself short."

"Okay, my turn again," Erin said. "It's funny. I ran into a young Irishwoman, thought you might know her. She had the same accent you do."

"Belfast's a large city," he said. "There's a great many would talk like me."

"Yeah, you'd remember her, though. Name of Siobhan. Siobhan Finneran."

Carlyle was a master of self-control. Erin was watching his eyes for the flicker of recognition or surprise, and she still almost missed it. But it was there.

"Where exactly did you encounter this lass?" he asked quietly.

She decided to play his game of answering a question with another question. "Where was she the last time you saw her?" she countered.

"The airport."

"So you do know her."

"You know I do," he said. "I'll not insult the both of us by claiming otherwise. I don't like to lie to you, Erin."

"I know you don't," she said. "You're good at telling technical truths."

He smiled grimly. "It's a skill one learns in my line of work. Now, why are you asking about Siobhan?"

"She was at the crime scene," Erin said.

"Tonight?"

"Yeah. Why would that surprise you?"

He shook his head. "I thought she was in Belfast."

"Hold on. You said you saw her at the airport."

"Aye," he said. "But I was dropping her off. She was on her way home, and that was some time ago. I've not seen her for five years, Erin."

She did some quick mental arithmetic. "How old is she?"

"She was nineteen at the time," he said. "She'd be twenty-four now."

"You left Ireland in, what, '95?"

"Aye."

"So she'd have been just a kid. Six years old?"

"Aye. Erin, what's your point?"

"Who is Siobhan? To you, I mean."

He sighed. "Cormac Finneran was a friend of mine. Good lad, good friend, good soldier."

"IRA?"

"Aye. We served in the same brigade. There were four of us: Cormac, Corky, Pat McDugan, and myself. Pat was young and mad, like Corky. Cormac was the old man of the lot, near forty years old. He'd a wife, a sweet colleen by the name of Iona."

Erin was astonished to find Carlyle so suddenly talkative. She decided to let him go and see where his reminiscences took them.

"The rest of us had no children. Or, in Corky's case, none that he knew of." Both of them had to smile at that. "Cormac had the one daughter, Siobhan. A lovely lass, the brightest green eyes you've ever seen. She was his pride and joy. He made the lot of us swear that if anything ever happened to him, we'd look after her and Iona. We'd not refuse him, of course. All of us loved the lass. She was a sort of mascot to us, such a fine, cheerful girl, always asking questions, watching what we were doing. She was smart as a whip, too. Show her something once, and she could do it herself."

He sighed again. "I suppose you've already guessed where this story's heading. In the summer of '94, some of our lads did away with a member of the UVF on Shankill Road."

Erin nodded. She knew about the Ulster Volunteer Front, a Protestant paramilitary group that, though supposedly on the side of the British, was really as much of a terrorist group as the IRA they were fighting. If anything, they were worse.

"In return, the UVF did their usual business, which was to go into a Catholic pub and gun down whatever poor lads they found there. Civilians, of course. They'd not be likely to face off against our lads head-on." Carlyle laughed bitterly. "As it turned out, though, Cormac was in that pub taking a pint. They didn't even know he was one of ours. Not that it mattered. Cormac was shot in the chest. He died before he even made it to hospital."

"So what happened to Siobhan and Iona?" Erin asked.

"We did what we could," Carlyle said. "I was just married myself, and Rosie and I tried to help. So did Pat. Even Corky pitched in, the closest brush with responsibility I think he's ever had. But Siobhan spent most of her time with Rosie and me.

"She missed her da very much. After a while, she even took to calling me father. But then Rosie was killed and…" he trailed off.

Erin, to her own surprise, laid her hand on his. "And what?" she asked quietly.

"The light went out of me," he said. "I scarcely knew what I was doing. I certainly couldn't look after a young lass. Iona saw it, too, and didn't like it. She didn't bring Siobhan around so often. She took up with Pat, and sure enough, the two of them married. It steadied him down a bit. There wasn't anything left for me there, so I came to the States."

"But you still saw Siobhan."

"Aye," he said. "Iona and Pat came over several times as the years went by. I watched Siobhan grow up. We exchanged letters. The old-fashioned kind, on pen and paper. She was always very interested in keeping in touch with me, more than Iona was." He picked up his empty glass, stared at it for a moment, then signaled Danny for a refill. He didn't say anything more until he'd taken another drink of whiskey.

"I should have stayed, for her sake," he finally said. "Her mum didn't want her around me, but I think that was a mistake. She'd just lost her da, she didn't need to lose me as well. Perhaps she'd have turned out better if—"

He stopped. "Well, things went as they did," he finished. "No point crying over the past, aye?" He took another sip of Glen D. "And now you know what Siobhan is to me."

Erin nodded. She realized she still had her hand resting on Carlyle's and wasn't sure what to do with it. She ought to pull it back before things got awkward, but if she did it suddenly, that would call more attention to the gesture. She disguised her motion by raising her hand to get Danny's attention. "One more, if you don't mind," she said.

"Sure thing, Erin," Danny said with a grin.

While he was pouring the drink, she looked back at Carlyle. "Siobhan didn't turn out like you thought she should?" she asked.

"None of us are as good as we want to be," he said. "It's fortunate we've the Catholic church to shelter us poor sinners."

"She showed up in New York carrying a gun," Erin said. "At the scene where a police officer was shot. In a warehouse owned by the O'Malleys." She held up a hand. "I know, I know, you can't talk about that and I won't ask you about it. But she missed running into Hans Rüdel by just a few minutes."

"I was under the impression your department had declared Mr. Rüdel dead," Carlyle observed.

She snorted. "Are you going to tell me that news wasn't what brought Corky running in here this evening?"

"As I've said, Erin, I'll not insult the both of us by lying to you."

"I'm going to find Rüdel," Erin said. "I don't know what Siobhan has to do with this, but if she's involved, she's in trouble, and maybe in danger. Do you know why she was at the warehouse on Fletcher?"

"Nay," Carlyle said. "But I intend to find out."

Chapter 5

Erin didn't go back to the precinct. It was late, she'd had a long day, and they weren't going to close the case that night. She used to think detectives would work for days straight, living in the office on takeout food and sleeping on the couch in the break room. That didn't usually happen. Even the high-priority cases took days, sometimes weeks. Her dad liked to say that good police work was a marathon, not a sprint. So she went home.

She took Rolf for a quick turn around the neighborhood, gave him a late supper, and nuked a frozen dinner for herself. Then she settled down in front of the TV to try to shut off her brain for the evening.

She hadn't been sitting more than a minute or two when her building's front-door buzzer went off.

Erin jumped. She'd been a little high-strung ever since a serial killer had tried to murder her in her own dining room that July. "Take it easy," she said out loud as she got up and went to the intercom box. "Who is it?"

"It's Kira."

"What?"

"Kira. Kira Jones."

Erin shook her head, even though the other woman couldn't see her. "No, I heard you. I mean, what are you doing here?"

"We need to talk."

The sound quality through the intercom was terrible, but Erin could still tell something was a little off in Kira's voice. "Are you okay?"

"Yeah. It's just... can I come up?"

"Sure." Erin buzzed her in and spent the next half-minute wondering what the hell was going on. When she heard the knock on her door, she couldn't help getting a grip on her Glock while she checked through the peephole to make sure Kira was alone in the hallway. Then she unlocked the door and opened it.

"Hey," Kira said.

"Hey," Erin replied. "C'mon in. You want something to drink?"

"No, thanks." Kira stood in the entryway looking nervous.

"Come in, take a seat," Erin said, leading her to the living room. "We got something on the Hendricks case?"

"No." Kira didn't sit down.

"Jesus," Erin said. "You're making me twitchy. Is this work, or personal?"

"Neither. Both. Shit, I don't know." Kira ran a hand through her hair.

"You could've called," Erin said.

Kira shook her head. "No, I couldn't."

Now Erin was really confused. "Okay, is this about you, or about me?"

Kira took a deep breath. "It's about you."

Erin's mind raced. She leaned against the wall and tried to think what could possibly be going on. "Kira," she said, "I swear to God, if you don't start making sense in about five seconds, I'm gonna have to do something drastic."

"You were at the Corner, weren't you," Kira said. It wasn't a question.

"Yeah," Erin said. "Turns out Carlyle knows the Finneran chick. They go way back. He helped look after her in Ireland when she was a little girl. He claims he didn't know she was in New York, but I swear there's gotta be a connection. I think—"

"Erin, I don't care about that right now," Kira interrupted. "And neither will they."

"It means there's an O'Malley connection," Erin repeated. Then her brain caught up to the last thing Kira had said. "They?"

"IAB."

That was an NYPD officer's least favorite acronym. "Internal Affairs?" Erin said. "What the hell are you talking about?"

"They think there's a crooked cop at the Eightball," Kira said. "Someone dirty. Working for the O'Malleys."

Erin still didn't get it for a second. Then she did. It felt like taking a fist to the stomach. "They think it's me?" was all she could say.

"Think how it looks, Erin," Kira said. "You've been connected with Carlyle on two cases. You spend a lot of time there."

"There's nothing like that," Erin protested. "He's a contact, sure. But that doesn't mean—"

"It is just a business relationship," Kira said. "Isn't it? I mean, there isn't anything else going on?"

"Of course not!" Erin was getting pissed off, but her detective instincts were still working. "Hold on. IAB wouldn't tell you if they were investigating the squad. Unless..."

Kira looked away, suddenly finding Erin's living room carpet very interesting.

"You used to work Internal Affairs," Erin said. "Did they tap you for this? Shit, are you still working for them?"

It was Kira's turn to say, "It's not like that."

"What is it like, then? Because I'm having a hard time understanding this. Who came to you on this?"

"Lieutenant Keane."

That figured. Keane was head of IAB at Precinct 8. "And he asked you about me?"

"Yeah."

"Great. Fantastic. While we're trying to find a cop-killer, our very own Bloodhound is sniffing around the detectives who're trying to catch the bastard. God damn it, what the hell were you thinking, talking to IAB about me?"

Kira looked up at that, anger sparking in her own eyes. "I didn't make this happen, Erin. I didn't ask for it. I'm trying to help you here."

"What have you told them?"

"The truth. What did you think I'd say?"

"I thought you'd have my back!"

"I do have your back!"

They were shouting at each other now, glaring across Erin's living room. Erin wondered how things had gotten so bad. She was scared, that must be it. She remembered another piece of advice from her dad.

"There's nothing wrong with fear," he'd told her. *"It can keep you alive. But it can also make you stupid. So be scared, but stay smart."*

She reminded herself to breathe, to take a second and step back. "Okay," she said, steadying her voice as much as she could. "Why'd you tell me this?"

"I couldn't stand you not knowing," Kira said. Her own anger flowed out of her, leaving her looking strangely deflated.

"So you came here to help me see the light?"

"I came here to warn you," Kira said. "Because I've got your back. IAB's sniffing around you. Don't give them anything."

"I'm not doing anything! There's nothing for me to give them!"

"If it even looks bad, they'll be all over you. You know how investigations go. Once they start looking, they want to find what they're looking for. Even if they call it off in the end, it could still screw your career."

"And you came here in person because…"

"If there's an official investigation, they'll have your phone records. Maybe a tap."

Erin felt foolish. She should've figured that out. "You didn't want to leave a record of this conversation."

Kira nodded. "To protect both of us."

"Shit," Erin said.

"Pretty much," Kira agreed.

"So what do I do?"

"Keep your nose clean and work the case."

"That's what I was going to do anyway."

"Should be easy, then."

"Yeah, easy," Erin snorted. "Looking over my shoulder the whole time."

"And stay away from the O'Malleys."

"We may need them to solve this thing."

"IAB's not gonna like that," Kira said.

Erin didn't quite have her anger under control yet. "I don't answer to them!"

"We all answer to them," Kira said. "You don't want to have Keane on your case. Seriously, Erin. He's bad news. Whatever you've heard about him, the truth is worse."

"So how long do I need to keep my head down?"

"I don't know. Until it blows over."

"When will that be?"

"I don't know," Kira said again.

Silence thickened the air between them.

"What if we find the O'Malleys' guy?" Erin said suddenly. "The real one."

Kira blinked. "So now you want to work for IAB?"

"I want to save my own ass," Erin retorted.

Kira thought it over for a moment. "Okay," she said.

"Okay what?"

"I'm in. Let's find the son of a bitch."

"I'm still pissed at you," Erin said.

"I get that." Kira smiled sourly. "I'd be pissed at me, too. But I really am trying to help you. I told Keane you weren't dirty."

"Did he believe you?"

"Have you ever talked to that guy? I've got no freaking idea what he's thinking."

"Great," Erin muttered. "Welcome to Paranoiaville."

"Yeah," Kira agreed. "Population: you, plus all the people who're out to get you."

* * *

Erin sat alone on her couch after Kira left. She had the TV on, but she didn't even see what was on the screen. She was trying to think. Everything kept coming back to the O'Malleys, and they were exactly the people Kira had told her to stay away from. How the hell was she supposed to solve the case?

The crazy thing was, her first thought was to talk to Carlyle, get his take on things. He certainly had some experience in dealing with police inquiries from the other side. He'd understand, and would probably even have some good advice.

She needed to get her head screwed on straight. To do that, she needed help. But not from inside the department. At least, not the current department. Erin knew one guy who'd had contact with the O'Malleys while wearing a shield, and he'd stayed clean. She turned off the TV and picked up her phone.

"O'Reilly," the man on the other end of the line answered.

"Hey, Dad," she said.

"Hey, kiddo! You in trouble?"

Sean O'Reilly, retired NYPD Patrol officer, always felt the need to make sure Erin was okay when she called him. Her normal response was a quick, cheerful reassurance. This time she hesitated.

"I don't know," she said, knowing he'd already started worrying.

"What do you need?" he asked. His voice shed years of retirement in an instant. He was all police, all business.

She hesitated again, wondering whether her phone was really tapped. Paranoiaville, she thought ruefully. "It's not an emergency. But I need to work some stuff out. You heard about the officer shooting?"

"I heard." One of Sean's old friends was a desk sergeant at Precinct 8. "You catch the case?"

"Yeah. We already know who did it. It's the guy Vic shot on the docks."

"The German hitman?"

"Yeah."

"I thought he was dead."

"So did we. I'll fill you in on the details later. The main thing is, he was working with the O'Malleys before."

"I remember," Sean said. Erin had given him some info on the case back when she'd thought it was closed. "You thought one of them hired him to take out an internal competitor. Morton Carlyle was the target."

Sean was a good fifteen years older than Carlyle, but he'd known Carlyle when the Irishman was young, fresh off the boat. They hadn't been friends, but they hadn't exactly been enemies either. Sean had never trusted him and didn't particularly like Erin having contact with him.

"That's right," Erin said. "And we found a person of interest at the scene, another O'Malley associate. A woman, Irish-born. Acquaintance of Carlyle's."

"Is that a guess on your part?"

"He confirmed he knew her."

"I'm surprised you got that out of him."

"He didn't know she was in town. I caught him off guard."

Sean whistled. "You're the first one I ever heard who managed that with Cars." He paused. "Wait a second. He didn't know she was there?"

"I don't think so."

"So what's going on?"

"Damned if I know," Erin said. She reflexively followed up, "Sorry." Old habits died hard, and when she'd been a little girl she'd have gotten a scolding for bad language.

"But it sounds like you've got some leads," Sean said. "What's your trouble?"

She sighed. Her dad wasn't going to like what came next. "I've gotten some info on a couple of cases from Carlyle. He's become kind of an unofficial CI."

"Erin, I warned you about him, and guys like him."

"I know, Dad." She rolled her eyes. This sounded a lot like a conversation he'd had with her about sports jocks when she'd been in high school. "He's been playing straight with me. We're on good terms."

"You sure about that?"

"Yeah. I am."

"You sure he's not playing you?"

"He's not playing me!"

He let it go. "Okay, so you've got an in on the case. Use it."

"That's the problem."

"I don't copy."

"The way things have been going, I'm worried about how it's going to look if I work too closely with one of the O'Malleys."

"You worried about your squad or your boss?"

"Neither."

"IAB?"

She closed her eyes. "Yeah."

There was a long pause.

"Erin?" he asked quietly.

"Yeah?"

"They aren't going to find anything if they look, are they?"

"Dad, I'm not dirty!"

"That's not what I meant." But it was, and they both knew it. That question was still hanging between them.

"I gotta solve this thing, Dad," she said at last. "What if I need Carlyle to do it?"

"He can probably help you," Sean said. His voice was strangely flat. "He saved my career once. But be careful, because there's going to be a price. Don't sit down at the table with more than you're prepared to lose."

"You worry too much, Dad."

"You're my only daughter. I worry exactly the right amount."

She managed a little laugh, but it was forced. "I better go. I'll catch you later."

"Let me know how it turns out, kiddo. Take care of yourself."

"Always do, Dad."

Chapter 6

Erin didn't get much sleep, but she rolled out of bed ready to get back to work. Anything was better than sitting around worrying. After her usual morning run, shower, and a quick breakfast, she and Rolf went to the precinct.

Kira was already there, bent over her computer screen. The others hadn't arrived yet. Erin got a cup of coffee from the break room. They'd received an anonymous donation of a brand-new espresso machine earlier that year, which had improved morale but had also led to a bunch of other officers hanging around Major Crimes until Captain Holliday had ordered them to knock it off. It was unspoken knowledge in the unit that the machine had been a little thank-you from Morton Carlyle for protecting his pub. To acknowledge it would have meant returning the gift, so everyone pretended they didn't know where it had come from.

"Hey, Erin," Kira said. She darted a quick, pleading look Erin's way, asking her to pretend everything was normal between them.

"Hey," Erin said, playing along. "Got anything?"

"Rüdel's face went out on the ten-o-clock news. Since then, we've had sixty-four sightings reported."

Erin sighed. "Any confirmed?"

"Nope. I'm collating them now, seeing if there's a pattern." Kira pointed to her computer screen, which showed a patchwork of red dots overlaid on a map of Manhattan. "We complain the community doesn't support us, then a high-profile case comes down and Joe Citizen starts seeing bad guys around every corner. I don't think we can filter out the random noise, but I'm trying."

"Wait a second," Erin said, pointing. "That can't possibly be right."

"I know," Kira said with a short laugh. "That's the Civic Center. Number One PP."

"Police Headquarters," Erin said. "Someone seriously reported him there?"

"Yeah. A guy said he saw Rüdel outside. Of course, by the time he got back out there with a couple officers, there was no sign of him." Kira rolled her eyes.

"At least it was creative," Erin said.

"You know, John Dillinger visited the Chicago Police Department while he was Public Enemy Number One," Kira said. "*Four times.* He saw his own picture on the wall."

"Maybe," Erin said. "But that was before cell phone cameras."

"Morning, ladies," Webb said, coming out of the elevator.

Kira glanced at Erin. "He talking to us?"

She shrugged. "Morning, sir."

"You going to make me the happiest detective in the Five Boroughs?"

"Don't think they're paying me enough for that," Kira said.

"Nothing yet?" Webb asked, hanging up his coat and coming over to Kira's desk.

"Scattered sighting reports," Kira said. "Nothing definite."

"He's still here," Webb said. "I'd bet my shield on it. And if he is, we'll get him. He's not a New York native. He can't stay underground forever."

"He can if we put him there," Erin said.

Webb gave her a sour smile. "I'd like nothing better. He's a cop-killer, armed and dangerous, so maybe it'll come to that. But remember, if we get the chance to take him without loss of life, including his, that's what we're going to do. This is police work. We're not violent thugs."

"Yes, sir," Erin said.

"Speaking of which," Webb said, "where the hell is Neshenko?"

"Don't know," Kira said.

Webb pulled out his phone. "Detectives are like cats," he grumbled while he poked at the screen. "Good hunters, but just try to get them all pointed the same direction. Neshenko? Oh good, you're still alive. Where are you? *Where?* Brooklyn? What's in Brooklyn? You don't think that's a waste of your time and the City of New York's taxpayer dollars? No, go ahead. Take your time. Why don't you catch a game at Citi Field while you're at it? But maybe next time you might think of telling your commander where you're going." He hung up and put his phone away.

"What's going on?" Erin asked.

"He's at the docks where Rüdel was shot the first time around," Webb explained. "He thinks there might be some sort of clue there."

"As to where Rüdel is now?" Erin said, her skepticism coming out in her voice.

Webb spread his hands. "How the hell am I supposed to know that? Please tell me one of you has a better idea how to find this asshole before he kills someone else."

"I'd like to go back to the warehouse," Erin said. "Look over the scene again, see if I can figure what he was doing there."

"Laying low, probably," Kira said. "The O'Malleys were sheltering him before."

Erin shook her head. "I don't think so. The place was broken into. If Rüdel was there with permission, who broke in the door?"

"The Finneran chick maybe," Webb suggested.

"That'd mean she was there before the shooting," Erin said. "Michaelson said they saw signs of a break-in. That was why they stopped in the first place."

"Right," Webb said. "You think the O'Malleys are still fighting each other?"

"Maybe," she said. "I'd like to take another run at Finneran, too."

"Can't," Webb said. "Her lawyer got her released about two in the morning."

"You just let her go?" Erin exclaimed.

"What exactly would you recommend I charge her with?" he retorted.

Erin clenched her fists, feeling her fingernails dig into her palms. "Okay, whatever. I still want to take another walk around the scene, see if anything pops."

"Okay," Webb said. "But be ready to get back here the second you hear from me. If we get a credible report, we're going to go wheels-up pretty fast."

"Hang on a sec," Kira said. "I'll come with you."

"Okay."

*   *   *

They took Erin's car, since Kira's Taurus didn't have a compartment for Rolf. They didn't say anything on the way down to the garage.

"So, I was thinking about what we talked about last night," Erin finally said as they pulled out of the garage and turned south.

Kira shook her head and put a finger to her lips.

Erin realized the other woman thought her car might have been bugged by Internal Affairs. The sheer craziness of it distracted her and almost made her coast through a red light. She jammed on the brakes and heard irritated honking from the car behind her, who'd apparently decided to run the light on her tailpipe.

"It's just hard to know where Rüdel's going if we don't know what he wants," she said, trying to pretend that was what she'd been considering all along.

"The CSU guys will have gone over the whole place," Kira said. "I'm not sure what you're hoping to find."

"Clarity," Erin said.

"You want that, you shouldn't have joined the NYPD," Kira said. "You should've gone into the priesthood."

"You're not Catholic, are you?"

"My mom's a neo-Pagan Hippie, my dad's a lapsed Unitarian. Not sure what that makes me."

"The Catholic church doesn't ordain women," Erin reminded her. Then she blinked as Kira's words caught up with her. "How can he be a lapsed Unitarian? Is that even possible?"

Kira shrugged. "He used to think everything was part of the beautiful pattern of the universe, but now he doesn't, I guess."

*   *   *

The warehouse was sealed with about yellow police tape, more tape forming a square around the site of the shooting. CSU had cleaned things up pretty thoroughly. A few pebbles of shattered safety glass were all that was left where the squad car had been.

Erin had the urge to draw her gun on their way inside, which was silly. This site had been ransacked by criminals, then cleared by police officers, then gone over by crime-scene techs. There was no reason for anybody to be hanging around. It was just a symptom of how jumpy Kira had made her.

The interior of the warehouse looked about like it had the day before. CSU had scooped up the broken bits of the packing crate, but the other boxes still sat on their wooden pallets, unopened.

"Why didn't they check these?" Erin wondered.

"Intact customs seals," Kira said, pointing. "You'd need a warrant, and you'd never get one. After all, technically, these goods belong to a burglary victim."

"Right," Erin said. "Is there any rule you don't know?"

"The Patrol Guide's over two thousand pages long. I haven't memorized it all." Kira paused. "Yet."

"You really think they're bugging my car?" Erin asked, bending over to look at the customs information on the nearest crate.

"You want to take the chance?"

"I told you before, I didn't do anything!"

"And I told you, that doesn't matter once they get looking. You can still get hurt."

"How could you do it?" Erin said, straightening up and looking her fellow detective in the eye.

"Do what?"

"Work IAB. Spy on your own people."

"Someone's got to. There has to be accountability. Otherwise we're just another street gang."

Erin thought of some of her dad's stories. "That's pretty much what the NYPD was in the beginning."

"You want to go back to that? Draft Riots, Tammany Hall, all that bullshit? Erin, do you really want dirty cops to get away with it?"

"Of course not! I told you that!"

"Then what do we do? Either we have independent civilian oversight, or we have to take care of things ourselves through Internal Affairs."

"But who watches Internal Affairs?"

"Oh, for Christ's sake, Erin! You have to stop watching the watchmen somewhere."

"I don't like it," Erin said. "Any of it."

"I kinda miss IAB sometimes," Kira said quietly.

"Why?"

"For one thing, no one ever took a shot at me there."

"No one shoots at IA. They just sit behind desks and dream up ways to stab real cops in the back," Erin said. She squatted beside another crate. "These boxes are from Scotland."

"Okay," Kira said. "What's in them?"

"According to the description of contents, it's petrochemicals. There's warning labels on some of these."

"But not explosives?"

"Rolf doesn't think so," Erin said. "The nose knows."

Rolf showed no interest at all in the crates. He was watching Erin, waiting for instructions.

"You remember when we went after Rüdel this summer?" Erin asked.

"As I recall, you and Vic got shot at. Again."

"There was an arms smuggler in Scotland, the boss of those two guys who got killed on the boat. Smiling Jack."

"Right," Kira said. "You're not telling me that's the name on the shipping labels, are you?"

"No," Erin said. "But I'm thinking it's quite a coincidence, Rüdel showing up to steal more Scottish explosives disguised in a cargo shipment."

"We ought to find Smiling Jack," Kira said.

"Yeah. Unfortunately, he's in Scotland, as far as I know. How big is our travel budget?"

"We could maybe ship you air freight," Kira said. "How much do you weigh?"

"None of your damn business."

"Erin, we can't go to Scotland."

"So we need to talk to someone who can, or someone who has connections there."

"Oh, God. Why do I get the feeling you're gonna say..."

"Carlyle."

"God damn it, Erin!"

"What? What! Tell me he can't help!"

"He won't!"

"I think he will."

"Your ass is gonna burn for this, you know."

"It's his ass, too," Erin reminded her. "Rüdel killed four of his guys. *Four*. Almost got Carlyle himself, too."

"Look," Kira said, suddenly looking very tired. "You can't go in there alone, not with Keane on your trail. I'll go with you."

"So you can tell the Bloodhound if I step out of line?"

Kira flinched.

Erin instantly regretted her words, but couldn't think of a good way to walk them back. "Okay, come along, if you insist. But Carlyle's not likely talk in front of someone he doesn't know."

"And he knows you?"

"A little. Enough."

"We done here?"

Erin looked around one more time, trying to see with a detective's eyes. Nothing sparked. "I think so. Let's go."

Chapter 7

The Barley Corner did some business at breakfast, but was pretty dead by mid-morning. Even most of the serious alcoholics didn't wrap themselves around their bottles before ten. The pub was almost completely empty when Erin, Kira, and Rolf walked in. Carlyle and Corky were both there, along with a half-dozen tough-looking guys who were probably O'Malley muscle.

Carlyle, always the gentleman, stood up when he saw the women enter. He said something in Corky's ear. Then he smiled at them, and it looked sincere, but Erin saw something a little more guarded than usual, like thin shades had been drawn just behind his eyes.

"Top of the morning, Detective O'Reilly, Detective Jones," he said.

"Mr. Carlyle," Erin said, matching his tone. "Mr. Corcoran."

"Please, Erin," Corky said with a grin. "Not even my old man was ever called that. It's Corky to you, now and forever. And to you, too, love," he added, turning his attention on Kira. "You don't mind if I call you Kira, do you?"

"I don't think I know you well enough for that," she said.

"Well, that's something we shall have to remedy," he said. "Now, I've no doubt you're here on official business, and it's a mite early for strong spirits regardless, but you'll not object to my buying you a fine cup of coffee and sharing a drink with me."

"I'm working, Mr. Corcoran."

"Of course you are, love." Corky moved closer and laid a hand lightly on Kira's shoulder. She twitched in reflex; police officers didn't like persons of interest initiating physical contact. But Corky had a disarming quality about him and she relaxed almost immediately. "Have you eaten recently?" he went on. "They make a lovely Ulster Fry here, or oatmeal if you've a hunger for something simpler. That's a fine thing you've done with your hair, by the by. That shade of blue brings out the shine in your eyes."

"Corky, you could at least wait to flirt with my coworkers until I'm not around," Erin said.

"Love, I'm afraid once the train's gone from the station, and you left alone on the platform, you've no say in what stops it makes," Corky said cheerfully. "You had your chance, left my heart broke and bleeding. I've moved on."

"What's he talking about?" Kira asked sharply.

"We had a torrid love affair in his imagination," Erin said.

"Not entirely," Corky said with a wink.

"Remember it however you want to," she retorted.

"I can see when I'm not appreciated," Corky said. "Kira, love, I can see she's filling your head with all manner of terrible things about me. At least give me the chance to convince you otherwise."

Kira, torn between annoyance and amusement, let Corky lead her partway down the bar to ply her with caffeine. Carlyle and Erin watched them for a few moments.

"He doesn't give up easy, I'll give him that," Erin remarked. But as she said it, she wondered. He actually seemed to have given up on her, which was another unusual thing.

"Oh aye, he's tenacious," Carlyle agreed.

"He's also running interference for you."

"Why would you say that?"

"You haven't called me Detective O'Reilly in months. You knew we were here officially, and you didn't want to talk to both of us together. So he cut her loose from me."

"You think he's not really interested in her?"

"She's female, and breathing, so yeah, he's interested," Erin said. "But that's not the main point. That's just a bonus."

Corky said something, the punchline of a joke, and Kira burst out laughing.

"The lad means no harm," Carlyle said, then went on in a lower voice. "But why didn't you come alone?"

"It's official, like I said," Erin replied, also speaking quietly. "We pair up most of the time when we're working cases."

Carlyle shook his head. "I don't assist you in an official capacity, Erin. You know that."

"This is serious," she said. "I know what was in the box Rüdel found at the warehouse. Don't you?"

"If I don't know which box you're referring to, I'd have no way of knowing what he took," Carlyle returned.

"We may not have much time," Erin said. "I know it was one of Smiling Jack's special packages. And why the hell is your organization moving explosives, anyway?"

"Businesses provide what their customers want," Carlyle said. "That's the very foundation of economics."

"I need specifics," Erin said. "How much, what kind of explosives. I have to know why Rüdel wanted them, how he knew about them, and what he's planning to do with them."

"I don't know the answers to everything you're asking," Carlyle said. "If I did, I might not be at liberty to tell you. But I can tell you this. Hans Rüdel is not working for Evan O'Malley. In point of fact, Evan's quite as displeased as New York's finest that the lad is still running about. But he assures me that situation will resolve itself presently."

"Oh, that's comforting," Erin said. "Do you know who Rüdel's working for now?"

"I'm not aware that he's engaged under any of the O'Malleys."

"But he was. Before."

"I believe so, aye."

"By someone who wanted to eliminate you."

"Aye."

"Who?"

"Erin," he said with a more genuine smile. "Why are you wanting my help when you're nine-tenths of the way to your destination?"

"You can't make it easy, can you."

"Would you want me to?"

"It'd make a nice change, once in a while," she said. "But I need something on Smiling Jack. Somehow, Rüdel knows about his shipments."

"I'm aware of that," Carlyle said. "Some of our lads have been asking the same question. Let me make some inquiries. Come after closing tonight, to the back door. Two-thirty. My lads will let you in. Then we'll talk."

"You know more than you're telling me," she said. "Talk to me now."

"I'll talk," he said, "but only to you." He tilted his eyes Kira's direction. The other woman was still listening to Corky with half an ear, but she kept glancing at Erin and Carlyle.

"I don't know if I can," she said.

Carlyle's eyes narrowed. "Are you in trouble?" he asked in a still lower voice.

Nineteen times out of twenty, Erin would have said she was fine. What she said was, "I don't know."

He nodded. "I thought as much. I'll do what I can."

*   *   *

"Why was I even there?" Kira demanded the second the Corner's door closed behind them.

"You wanted to come," Erin reminded her.

"And Corcoran, he... I just... I can't believe that guy!" Kira said. "What's your story with him, anyway?"

"He made a move on me back when we were investigating that car bombing. I didn't know he was connected at the time. When I found out he was a mob guy, I called it off."

"Oh." Kira thought it over. "Well, I can see why you'd be interested. It's not that he's that handsome, exactly. He's got..."

"Charisma," Erin said. "So does Carlyle."

"You can say that again," Kira said. "Good-looking, too. And that accent. Whatever you think of the men, I'd sleep with the accent. Second-sexiest in the world."

"Says who?" Erin said sharply. Kira was right. Carlyle was a handsome man, but she didn't see the relevance to the case.

"I read a study."

"Of course you did."

"Carlyle give it up?"

"What?" For a disorienting second, Erin thought Kira was still talking about sex. Then she recovered. "He's looking into it, making calls. He'll get back to me."

"Someday maybe I'll understand why you trust him."

"I can't explain it," Erin said.

"I just hope you're right. You could get hurt."

"What about our other problem?" Erin asked, changing the subject.

"The O'Malley mole?"

"You're the IA cop. Any bright ideas?"

Kira shrugged. "We start by building a map of the organization, then we cross-check cases and duty rosters to find connections. Problem is, we don't know how long our guy's been compromised. Or even if he exists. Keane could be wrong. Maybe there isn't a mole."

"Keane have a history of being wrong?"

"Not so much."

"So, back to the precinct?"

"Might as well," Kira said. "I can get started on the O'Malley file. Might help us find Rüdel, too. You never know."

*   *   *

The rest of the day went by slowly. Webb and Erin were on the phone most of the time, talking to people who were nearly sure they might have seen a guy who looked kind of like Rüdel. They plotted more red dots on Kira's diagram. But nothing was completely credible, and all they had to show for it was a map of Manhattan that looked like it had a bad case of chicken pox. Vic came in after a couple hours in Brooklyn, tired and pissed off. His mood didn't improve when Webb put him on the phone with Scotland Yard to try to find out about Smiling Jack.

However, he was the only one of them who came up with anything concrete to add to the whiteboard in the department. The squad gathered around after he'd finished talking to the British detectives to see what he had.

"Smiling Jack's real name is John James McDonnell," Vic said. "He's a nasty piece of work from Glasgow."

"Glaswegian," Kira said, taking the opportunity to improve her comrade's vocabulary.

Vic gave her a look. "From Glasgow," he repeated. "He receives and transports stolen goods, especially weapons. Specializes in military hardware, the real serious stuff. Sniper rifles, machine-guns, rocket launchers—"

"*Rocket launchers?*" Webb echoed incredulously.

"Apparently he's got contacts in the British military," Vic said. "Anyway, they're looking at him for a job at an arms depot, the Kinloss Barracks. It's a Royal Engineers facility. Sounds like they misplaced some plastic explosives."

"How much?" Erin asked.

"About a thousand kilos."

"Jesus Christ," Webb muttered.

"That's a lot," Erin said. "If that was all at the warehouse..."

"That son of a bitch could blow up a sizable building," Vic said.

"That's not my point," Erin said. "How'd he get it out of the warehouse?"

"Getaway vehicle," Vic said.

"I don't think so," Webb said. "Michaelson would've mentioned that. And they weren't carrying that much when they shot Hendricks. A thousand kilos... if Rüdel just had himself and the other two guys, that's a lot of weight per man. Multiple trips."

"So where did they go?" Erin asked. "And where are the bombs?"

"Those are damn good questions," Webb said. "I want to talk to Michaelson. Holliday sent him home, so that's where we'll go. O'Reilly, you're with me. You drive."

*　　*　　*

Michaelson lived in an apartment on the Lower East Side of Manhattan. As Erin drove through the neighborhood, she pointed to another apartment building.

"I live there," she said.

"That so?" Webb said without much interest.

"Yeah. Michaelson heard about the vacancy, got me the spot. Great deal, too."

"Probably the last tenant died, Michaelson responded and knew it'd open up for a new tenant," Webb said.

Erin made a face. "Thanks for that thought, sir."

"How else does a Patrol officer learn about open real estate?" Webb replied.

At Michaelson's building, Webb rang him from the lobby. It took so long for a reply that Erin figured he was out, or maybe sleeping late, but finally Michaelson's voice came out of the speaker.

"What the hell do you want?"

Even through the tinny sound of the intercom, Erin heard the flat, dead note in the man's words.

"It's Harry Webb, Bob," Webb said. "I'm sorry, but I need to talk to you about the shooting. I've got Erin O'Reilly with me, and her little dog, too."

Michaelson didn't laugh. "It's not a good time, Lieutenant."

"I know it isn't," Webb said. "But we need to go over things again."

"What's the point? I told you what happened."

"You want us to catch the bastards who killed Hendricks?" Webb asked.

"Okay, whatever," Michaelson said and opened the lobby door.

He lived on the fourth floor, so they took the elevator. Webb adjusted his necktie while they took the ride upstairs.

"Sir, was that necessary?" Erin said. Her boss was being pretty harsh on a man who'd just lost his partner. She'd had an officer die in her arms once, so she knew the feeling. It wasn't something you bounced right back from.

"Michaelson knows the game," Webb said, not looking at her. "I'm a detective, not a damned grief counselor. You want to hold his hand, fine. I'm going to catch that son of a bitch Rüdel and see him fry. Michaelson's going to thank me in the end."

"Sir, don't take this the wrong way," Erin said. "But you can be a real prick sometimes."

"That's why they made me a lieutenant."

Michaelson met them at his apartment door. He was wearing a set of NYPD sweats and a five o'clock shadow. His eyes were bloodshot with dark bags under them.

"C'mon in," he said.

Erin's police reflexes kicked in when they walked into the place. She was sure he hadn't left the apartment since getting home the day before. She smelled stale mac and cheese as they passed the kitchen. Dirty dishes were on the counter. There was an empty Kentucky Wild Turkey bottle in the trash, but no shot glasses in sight, which meant he'd been drinking straight from the bottle. There was no sign of another inhabitant.

"How you holding up, Bob?" Webb asked.

Michaelson shrugged.

"You get any sleep?"

"Not much."

Erin said, "I'm real sorry, man," and put her hand on his shoulder.

"Thanks," Michaelson said absently.

"Why don't we sit down and talk?" Webb suggested.

They settled around the coffee table in the living room. Michaelson had an odd assortment of old furniture. Erin sank into a maroon armchair that was too big for her, Webb perched on a bare wooden rocker, and Michaelson sat on a worn leather couch with stuffing poking out a corner. Erin couldn't help noticing Michaelson's service pistol on the table, a Glock 17 just like hers.

"You said Rüdel and his guys were carrying duffel bags," Webb said. He'd read Michaelson's statement enough times to memorize it.

"Yeah, black ones."

"How big?"

Michaelson held up his hands about three feet apart. "Like this."

"Heavy?"

"Yeah, they were carrying them like they were full."

"But they had free hands for shooting," Webb said. "Did they put the bags down to shoot?"

"No," Michaelson said. "Only Rüdel shot, the other two didn't even stop moving. He used one hand."

"And when he fired, you hit the deck?"

"Yeah. I hadn't got my gun unholstered yet. I was calling the 10-13 from behind the car."

"So you didn't see where they went?"

"Around the corner of the building, I guess."

"You guess, or you know?" Webb asked.

Michaelson shook his head. "That's the only way they could've gone. If they'd crossed the street or come by my car I'd have seen them."

"And you didn't pursue?" Webb asked.

"I was giving Tim first aid."

"How fast did the first units respond?"

"I don't know."

"Bob," Webb said softly. "I need you to do better than that."

"Three or four minutes."

"Did any cars roll out from your area between the shots and when your backup arrived?"

Michaelson shook his head again. "No."

"You might've heard them, out of sight?" Webb suggested.

"No. Not nearby. There were cars all over FDR, but it doesn't have access from Fletcher."

"So they were on foot? Why didn't someone spot them? Three guys, carrying big duffel bags and probably guns?" Webb wondered out loud.

"The hell do I know?" Michaelson retorted.

Erin caught Webb's eye. "Sir, you can't carry a thousand kilos in three duffels."

"I know," Webb said.

"A thousand kilos of what?" Michaelson said. "Cocaine?" He laughed hollowly. "At least then I know Tim died for twenty million bucks worth of drugs."

"We're not sure what was in the bags," Webb said. "But if there was that much weight, they'd have needed to take multiple trips."

"Right," Erin said. "But then why didn't they have a vehicle right there at the warehouse?"

"There anything else you need from me?" Michaelson interrupted. "Because I'd kind of like to be alone right now."

"No, that's fine, Bob," Webb said, standing up. "Thanks for your help. We're gonna nail this guy."

"If you say so," Michaelson said. "You know when Tim's funeral is?"

"Tuesday afternoon," Webb said. "Two o'clock. See you there."

"Yeah," Michaelson said.

"You take care of yourself," Webb said.

Michaelson shrugged.

* * *

In the hallway outside the apartment, Webb scratched his head. "I can't figure it," he said. "Where did the bastard go? And how did he move more than a ton of explosives on foot?"

"He couldn't," Erin said. "Michaelson must've missed something. If they had a getaway vehicle already running, he might not have heard the engine."

"I guess so," Webb said, but he wasn't convinced. "Maybe this wasn't the missing British plastique. Or maybe not all of it. Might have just been a portion, enough for three men to carry. We don't know enough yet.."

"Back to work?" Erin said.

Webb sighed. "Back to work."

Chapter 8

There wasn't much to do but wait. As far as the world was concerned, Hans Rüdel had dropped clean off the face of it. The squad did what they could, but there was no way to track the German. With one good sniff, Rolf could track him. Unfortunately, they didn't have anything with Rüdel's scent. So many people had been through the warehouse, there was no way the dog could pick him out from the rest. Webb and Vic went back to the crime scene anyway to knock on doors again, but they didn't have high hopes.

Erin passed the time helping Kira organize data. They'd gotten the O'Malley file from the Organized Crime Task Force and were building spreadsheets. Kira was a big fan of spreadsheets.

"If I'd wanted to look at these all day, I'd have gone to business school like Michael," Erin said, talking about her second brother.

"You could've stayed in Patrol," Kira said.

"Yeah, because we never had to fill out any paperwork there."

"Sarcasm is unladylike."

"But a gun and a bulletproof vest aren't?"

They called it a day a little after five. They could've pulled overtime, but there wasn't much point. Thirty-five thousand police were keeping their eyes open for Rüdel. His face was all over the TV and Internet. He couldn't have just disappeared, and it was driving Erin crazy, but her only lead was Carlyle, and he was still working his sources.

So she went home, walked Rolf, microwaved a frozen dinner, and tried to get some sleep. It was impossible. She was too distracted. Eventually she ended up watching cheesy cop shows on TV, trying to make her brain shut itself down. The hours crawled by.

What she really wanted was a drink. But that was a terrible idea. Actually, the whole thing was a terrible idea. Kira had specifically warned her not to talk to Carlyle alone. But what the hell gave Kira the right to tell her that? Erin was trying to solve a case, an important one. This wasn't something she was doing for the fun of it. She wasn't dirty, and Carlyle's insights could be valuable. So what did it matter if it looked like something else was going on between them? Let Internal Affairs do what they did. They wouldn't find anything on her.

Her digital clock appeared to be broken. The number hadn't moved for at least five minutes.

No, the clock was working fine. It blinked from 10:02 to 10:03.

Erin did some search training with Rolf. She had a few small samples of explosive residue, which she hid around her apartment. Rolf dutifully sniffed them out, got told what a good dog he was, and enjoyed gnawing on his chew-toy reward.

She went back to bed and lay there forever.

Finally, the clock showed two o' clock. She jumped up and got ready to go out.

Erin had been thinking about what to bring with her. She didn't wear her vest. Carlyle would notice it, and he'd think it showed lack of trust. But she strapped on both her guns, the Glock at her belt and the backup snub-nosed revolver in her ankle holster. And she took Rolf with her. Just in case. She wasn't vain, but she still took the time to dab on enough makeup to disguise the bags under her eyes.

The Corner was closed by the time she got there, as expected. She and her K-9 walked into the alley behind the pub and approached the back door. A security camera stared at her. She knocked, feeling like a spy in some second-rate thriller.

Heavy bolts clanked. The steel door swung open. A heavyset guy with a square face looked her over.

"I've come to see Mr. Carlyle," she said.

"And you are?"

"Erin."

He nodded, stepped back, and motioned her in. As he did, the flap of his jacket opened a little and she saw a hand cannon in a shoulder rig, a big .357 magnum. The moment she was inside, he closed and locked the door behind her.

The bar was dimly lit and almost deserted. Caitlin, the waitress, was flipping chairs upside down on tables. Two guys lurked in a corner booth. She wasn't surprised to see a pump shotgun on the table between them. That was a major weapons violation right there. She pretended not to notice it. Carlyle was nowhere in sight.

Erin turned to the big guy and cocked an eyebrow. He pointed straight up with one finger, his face carefully expressionless.

She went to the door to Carlyle's upstairs suite and knocked. Her knuckles made a muffled sound. The door wasn't just soundproofed, it was armored. But Carlyle had been waiting right on the other side, because he opened the door almost immediately.

"Evening, Erin," he said. "Do come in." Despite the lateness of the hour, he was as neatly dressed as always, down to his necktie and suit coat. He held the door politely. She and Rolf went inside and climbed the stairs to his apartment.

"You want to talk in the study?" she asked, hesitating at the top of the stairway.

"Nay, take your first right," he said. That doorway led to a living room, clean and well-furnished.

"Sit anywhere you please," he said. Erin picked the couch, which looked expensive and comfortable. She sat down and discovered she was at least half right.

"Can I get you anything to drink?" he asked.

"I shouldn't," she said. "I'm working."

"This is an unofficial conversation," Carlyle said. "Should anyone ask, I'll deny it took place. It's up to you, but I'll not be telling anyone."

She smiled. "I'm not supposed to be here at all."

"Really? Why do you say that?"

"Department protocol," she said quickly. She'd come awfully close to blurting out that there was an IA investigation into the O'Malleys. Even worse, she'd almost said it was because their relationship was right on the edge of being unprofessional. Damn it, she *did* trust Carlyle, more than she should. "What the hell," she went on, reaching for a distraction. "Gimme a drink."

"Any particular drink, or should I use my discretion?"

"Surprise me."

Carlyle had a small bar between the living room and kitchen. He busied himself with various ingredients, but his back was to her and she couldn't see what he was doing. After a moment, he came back with a pair of cocktail glasses filled with something red.

She took the glass from his left hand. He clinked the rim of the other glass against hers and sat down beside her on the couch, angled to face her.

Erin took a sip. "Manhattan cocktail," she guessed.

"That's right," Carlyle said. "I'd never drunk one until I came to this country. Do you know how cocktails became popular?"

"My dad always said it was during Prohibition," she said. "The bootleggers were using cheap booze, wood alcohol, that sort of stuff, and the vermouth and bitters camouflaged the taste."

"I've heard the same," he said. "I'm normally a whiskey lad, but none the worse for a change."

"So, what can you tell me?" she asked.

Carlyle took a drink and put his glass on the end table. His face was troubled. "We've a number of serious problems, Erin."

"Typical day for me," she said.

"There's naught typical about this," he said. "I imagine you've made inquiries of your own concerning the cargo that went missing from the warehouse."

"Yeah," she said. "How much of the plastique was there?"

"I'm taking a considerable risk discussing this with you," he said. "If your theory is correct regarding the missing crate, you'd be right in assuming it hadn't yet been distributed."

"All of it, then," she said with a sinking feeling in her gut.

Carlyle nodded. "So that's our first difficulty. A violent maniac is running about Manhattan with the knowledge and means to do a great deal of mischief."

"Do you know what he's planning?"

"Nay. That's the second problem. I've spoken to a lad I work with, and he's given me his personal assurance that clever Hans is under no orders from him, nor anyone working for him."

"Did he give you the same assurance after Rüdel tried to kill you last time?"

Carlyle smiled and even chuckled ruefully. "Nay, he didn't. He apologized for what he characterized as an unfortunate misunderstanding."

"Evan O'Malley sent Rüdel after you himself?" Erin exclaimed.

"That's another misunderstanding," Carlyle said. "Nay, Evan had naught to do with it. He apologized on behalf of his family."

Erin still didn't understand, and it showed on her face.

"His blood family," Carlyle elaborated. "We both suspect the same lad brought Rüdel into the country."

"Who was it?" Erin asked.

"Tommy Jay," Carlyle said. "Thomas J. O'Malley, that is. Evan's nephew. Which information I'll deny telling you, I needn't add."

"He's in your organization, too," Erin said.

"Aye."

"I'm surprised you'd give me his name."

"I know," Carlyle said, smiling again. "Code of silence and all that. Do remember, though, the lad tried to have me killed and nearly succeeded. At the moment I'm feeling no particular loyalty toward him. He should count himself lucky I've done nothing worse."

"But he's one of yours."

Carlyle's eyes flashed. "He's none of mine."

"But to go to the police?" Erin pressed.

"I'm not asking you to prosecute him," Carlyle said. "You needn't concern yourself with Tommy Jay."

Erin didn't like the sound of that. "We can get him," she said. "If we can prove a connection with Rüdel, we can get him on state and even Federal charges. He'd be off the street for good. Don't do anything stupid."

"I can't stop you from going after him, either," Carlyle said. "But I'd point out that Rüdel remains your more immediate problem."

"Any other problems I should know about?"

"Aye," he said. "I've been told your lads aren't the only ones attempting to remove Hans from circulation."

Erin had to play catch-up again, but she got there. "Holy shit," she said. "Evan's taken out a hit on Rüdel."

"Word on the street," Carlyle said, choosing his words as carefully as always, "is that should some misfortune befall Hans Rüdel, the one responsible will receive a generous windfall."

"How much?"

"The number fifty would be a reasonable approximation."

"This is a little weird," Erin admitted.

Carlyle raised an eyebrow. "How do you mean?"

"You're telling me your guys and mine are in a race to see who gets Rüdel first. This guy is screwed."

"That's likely true," Carlyle said. "But he may do considerable damage before he's discovered. None of us want that to happen. I'd like to suggest we pool our knowledge concerning the lad. We may be able to determine his target in time to prevent further loss of life."

"A former IRA bombmaker trying to stop a bombing," Erin muttered aloud. "I don't believe this shit."

"IRA policy was to minimize civilian casualties," Carlyle reminded her. "My lads liked to inform the British ahead of time when we intended to blow something up. Fifteen minutes' advance notice, generally."

This was, without a doubt, one of the strangest conversations of Erin's life. "Okay, let's try working together," she said, taking a slug of her cocktail. The alcohol no longer seemed like a bad idea. It might be the only thing getting her through this. "Do you think he'll make another try at you? Here at the Corner?"

"Nay," Carlyle said. "I was never anything but a paycheck to him."

"Who's paying him?"

"I've no idea. I believe he's freelancing."

"Then who's he out to get?"

Carlyle rubbed his chin. "I suppose he might feel resentful toward his former employer."

"Tommy Jay?"

"Aye. But I think not."

"Why not?"

Carlyle gave her a grim smile. "He'd not need a metric ton of explosives to dispatch a solitary Irishman. Tommy Jay's no hard target. Hans would simply put a bullet in the lad and be done. Nay, I suspect he's simply doing what any of us do when we meet with adversity."

"What's that?"

"He's falling back on what he knows best."

"Which is?" Erin was in no mood for games.

"You've read his police files," Carlyle said. "I've not seen them. What do they say about him?"

"He's a former neo-Nazi," she said. "He's got all these white-supremacist tats. He did a lot of anti-government stuff back in Germany. He's basically the German version of..." She trailed off. "Oh, shit."

Carlyle leaned forward and put a hand on her forearm. She hardly noticed. "What?" he prompted.

"Timothy McVeigh," she said quietly. "Rüdel's not a criminal, except to pay the bills. He's a terrorist."

Carlyle nodded. "You've struck on it, I fear. Now, we have to think what to do next. The best thing, of course, would be to find him. But if that's not possible, we may be able to deduce where he's going."

At that moment, Rolf sprang to his feet, facing the door. Startled, both Carlyle and Erin turned to look at the dog.

Siobhan Finneran stood in the doorway.

Chapter 9

It would have been hard to say who was more surprised. For about a second and a half the three people stared at each other. The Manhattan cocktail in Erin's stomach hadn't had time to seep into her bloodstream, so she couldn't blame the alcohol for her slowness. She'd simply been caught totally off her guard. Out of the corner of her eye she saw Carlyle, his mouth hanging half open. It was the first time she'd seen him truly lost for words.

Then the moment passed. Erin lunged off the sofa, landing on one knee and reaching for her Glock. Her half-empty cocktail glass tumbled, splashing a red stain on Carlyle's carpet. Rolf, sensing her alarm, sprang stiff-legged to her side, bristling. Siobhan sidestepped half behind the doorframe, her hand sliding inside her jacket, but seemed to change her mind and stood perfectly still.

Carlyle, hands held out, stepped between them. "Steady on!" he said sharply.

Erin's hand was on the grip of her pistol, her instincts screaming at her to get her gun up and fight for her life. This had to be a trap, a setup. But Carlyle was in her line of fire and she hesitated to throw down on him.

Then Siobhan smiled a girlish, mischievous little smile. "Mr. Carlyle," she said, moving her hand from her jacket up to the neck of her blouse. She twirled a stray strand of hair around her fingertip. "I do hope I've not interrupted anything."

"Not in the least, Siobhan," Carlyle said. "Though I confess I'm a trifle surprised to see you so late. You should have called, let me know you were in town."

"I thought I'd surprise you," she said. "And it was worth it. You should've seen the look on your face. You know, my da didn't think anything could rattle you."

Erin stood up carefully and holstered her Glock, but she kept her hand near it and watched Siobhan's hands. The first thing they taught you when you joined Patrol Division was to always watch the hands. "Evening," she said warily.

"Evening, Erin O'Reilly," Siobhan said. "Enjoying a little of New York's famous night life?"

"Ms. Finneran," Erin said. "Enjoying a little illegal entry?"

"Whatever entry's going on, it's surely not illegal," she said. "I've always been free to come and go anywhere this fellow calls home. Isn't that true, Uncle Cars?"

Uncle Cars? Erin thought.

"Aye," Carlyle said. "That's always been true, lass. Did Caleb let you in?"

"Aye, he did," Siobhan said. "Though it slipped his mind that you were already entertaining. We're all lucky I wasn't ten minutes later. It might have been a terrible embarrassment."

"I'm not sure I understand, lass," Carlyle said.

"Drinking cocktails with a colleen at two in the morning?" Siobhan said. "I wonder if you still think me the same wee innocent lass I was. I've grown up a bit, learned about the world." She cocked her hip to one side and rested a hand on it. "I'll wager I could even teach you a thing or two if you'd let me."

"I've no doubt," he said. "But what are you doing here now?"

"I'm working, love," she said. "Not at the moment, of course. I hadn't lined up a place to sleep. Last night the city was good enough to accommodate me." She shot a quick, sharp look Erin's way. "But I was hoping to crash the couch in your flat for a few hours. That was when I didn't know what furniture was spoken for."

"I was just leaving," Erin said, gritting her teeth.

Siobhan's eyes flashed maliciously. "I'm sure you were. Take care you don't leave any of your clothes behind."

"I've got everything I came with," Erin snapped. She glanced at Carlyle, but only for a second. She didn't want to take her attention off Siobhan. She'd been around a lot of criminals, and had a good sense of people. This woman was like old dynamite; dangerous and unstable. She was also certainly armed, but Erin couldn't frisk her in this situation. And she wasn't sure where Carlyle stood in this whole business. She was certain he hadn't known Siobhan was coming. He'd recovered his poise quickly, but she'd seen him thrown completely off his game for a second.

Carlyle returned her look. He didn't say anything, but his eyes were soft and open for a single breath. He was asking her to leave, to back down from the confrontation. She didn't understand, not completely, but she knew their conversation was over for the night.

"Thanks for the drink, Mr. Carlyle," she said, deliberately formal. "I'll see you later."

"Good night, Detective O'Reilly," he said, following her cue. "I'll see you out."

"That's okay," she said. "I know the way. Rolf, *komm*."

Siobhan stepped to one side to let her pass. "Cute pup," she commented.

Rolf ignored her completely, watching Erin for instructions. He had no idea what the humans were talking about, that wasn't his job. His job was to cover his partner, and he didn't trust this Irishwoman. His hackles were still raised as he stalked past Siobhan.

*   *   *

After a shot of adrenaline like that, there was no way Erin was getting to sleep. Even after the walk back to her apartment, she was still hopped up and wide awake. So she changed into her workout clothes and took Rolf for a three o'clock run, hoping it would clear her mind and wear out her body.

The exercise left her tired but no clearer. She took a shower and made herself go to bed anyway. She even managed to fall asleep for a couple hours.

Her alarm jolted her back awake. She sat bolt upright and groped for her gun before remembering she was safe in her own apartment. Her legs ached, her eyes burned, and her head throbbed. It was going to be one hell of a long day.

That thought was still fresh in her mind as she loaded Rolf into the Charger and started the engine. Her phone buzzed as she was buckling her seat belt. She saw an unidentified number and was immediately suspicious.

"Hello?" she said warily.

"Detective O'Reilly," said a familiar voice, one she couldn't immediately place.

"Who is this?"

"Lieutenant Keane."

Oh, shit, Erin thought. "Yes, sir?" was what she said.

"I understand you usually come into work about this time," he said. "If you can make the time, I'd like to speak with you before you clock in."

"I'm on my way to the precinct now," she said.

"There's a coffee shop on your way," he said. "It's called Wakeup Call. I'll meet you there. You could probably use a cup of coffee."

Did he know how she'd spent her night? She could've sworn she hadn't been followed. Paranoia sank its claws lovingly into the base of her spine. "I'll be there in a couple minutes," she said, trying to sound light and offhanded.

When she and Rolf walked into the shop, Keane was already there, seated at a booth by the front window. He looked alert and well-rested, his necktie perfectly knotted, the creases in his trousers ruler-straight. Two cups of coffee rested on the table in front of him.

"Cream, no sugar," he said by way of greeting.

"Yeah," she said, sitting down opposite him. She wasn't surprised he knew how she took her coffee, and wouldn't give him the satisfaction of being rattled by it. Rolf sat next to Erin and coolly eyeballed the IA lieutenant.

"Rough night?" Keane asked.

Erin was a little more unkempt than usual. Sleeping after a shower had left her hair a rumpled mess that she'd only partially tamed. She knew there were bags under her eyes and the headache was still there, pounding away.

"I've had worse," she said as brightly as she could. "The case is on my mind. It's tough when one of our own goes down."

"It is," Keane agreed. "Especially given your prior history, with the Brunanski incident."

"That's not affecting me," Erin said a little too quickly.

"You've been at Precinct 8 about three months now," he said. "How does detective work suit you?"

"It's fine."

"I hear you're good at it. Congratulations on your promotion, by the way."

"Thank you."

"How are you getting on with your squadmates?"

"Fine."

Keane smiled thinly. "I've always imagined being the mother of a teenager would be good practice for conducting police interviews."

"Is that what this is? An interview?"

"Just a conversation. Who on your team would you say you have the best relationship with?"

"Rolf."

Keane smiled again. It was a strange sort of smile. Everything about it looked genuine, but it was a distant thing, like Keane was amused at a joke only he got. "I'll rephrase. Which human member of your team are you on the best terms with?"

"I don't know. Vic, I suppose."

"Neshenko?" Keane raised his eyebrows in apparent surprise. "His jacket doesn't note him as being especially easy to get along with."

"We understand each other."

"Is that important to you?"

"It's good to know what to expect from your teammates."

"So you don't know what to expect from the rest of your team?"

"I didn't say that."

"Does it bother you talking to an Internal Affairs officer?"

"Should it?"

"We're on the same side, Erin."

"I'm glad to hear it."

"How's your coffee?"

"Fine." She hadn't touched it.

"How's Mr. Carlyle?"

He slipped the question in easily, nonchalantly. Erin tried not to react, but she could feel herself trying and knew he was watching her do it. Her hesitation felt very long. "He plays his cards pretty close," she said. "I don't really have him figured out."

"You've done very well as a detective so far," Keane said, pivoting subjects again. "Captain Holliday is very pleased. And I find your performance remarkable."

Keane had recommended Erin for her job after the Homicide detectives at her old precinct had reported her for insubordination. He just might have saved her career, and now he was subtly reminding her that she owed him one.

"I'm glad you're enjoying the show," she said.

"You do want to be careful of your emotions, though," Keane said. "If anything gets you into trouble, it won't be your brain."

"I'll keep that in mind."

"I continue to watch your progress with great interest. Please, if you ever need to discuss anything, get anything off your chest, don't hesitate to contact me. You have my number in your phone."

"I was raised Catholic, sir. When I need to get something off my chest, I go to confession."

"Do you feel the need to do that often?"

"That's between me, my priest, and God."

Keane's smile seemed a trifle more authentic, or maybe it was just her imagination. "Well, I'm sure you're eager to get your nose back to the grindstone. There's a killer to catch."

"There always is," she replied, standing up.

He stood along with her and held out his hand. "We're not monsters in IAB, Erin. I have your best interests at heart, you know."

"That's comforting," she said, shaking his hand. He had a firmer grip than she'd expected. He kept eye contact while they shook, not blinking. His eyes were very dark brown, almost black, and piercing.

"I'll be seeing you," he said.

She didn't doubt it.

*   *   *

Erin knew the squad hadn't made much progress from the moment she stepped onto the second floor. There was no energy in the air. Vic was hunched over a gigantic cup of Mountain Dew at his desk. Kira had her chin resting on her palm, looking at nothing in particular. Webb was leaning against the conference table, staring at an unlit cigarette and clearly wishing it was in his mouth.

"You're late, O'Reilly," Webb said without looking up.

"Yeah, I can see I missed a lot," she said. "Sir, we need to talk to the captain."

That got their attention. "What about?" Webb asked.

"I've got confirmation from a CI," she said. "It was the missing plastique at the warehouse. Rüdel's in the wind with enough explosives to take out an office building. And he's probably not working for anybody. We suspect he's planning some sort of terrorist attack."

"You sure about this, O'Reilly?" Webb asked. "Or is it one of your hunches?"

"Like the serial killer thing?"

"I know," he sighed. "You were right about that one. Okay, we'll brief the captain. This CI of yours, did he happen to give us anything we can use to find Rüdel?"

She shook her head.

"Didn't think so," Webb said. "Come on."

Captain Holliday's office was in the corner of the same floor as Major Crimes, so they only had a few yards to walk. The door was half open. Webb knocked lightly on it. "Sir?" he called.

"Come in," Holliday said.

He had his phone against his ear when they entered. "Yes, sir," he said. "I understand. I'll let you know if we need anything else. Thank you, Commissioner." He hung up and looked at Erin, Webb, and Rolf.

"How bad is it?" he asked, taking in the detectives' expressions.

"O'Reilly, give it to him straight," Webb said.

Erin laid out what she knew without saying anything that would compromise her source. Holliday rubbed his mustache thoughtfully while she talked, letting her go on without interrupting. When she finished, he nodded. "Anything else?"

"No, sir."

"How credible is your CI?"

"He's well-connected in the underworld," she said. "And I don't think he's ever lied to me."

"Who is he?"

"I can't say that, sir. If it became known he was giving us information, it would get him killed."

Holliday nodded again. "I just got off the phone with the PC. I'll call him back and encourage him to take this Federal. We've got a lot of eyes on us, Detectives. What leads do we have?"

"We're exploring a variety of avenues," Webb said.

Holliday held up a hand. "Spin management is my job in this precinct. When you come in this office, check the bullshit at the door."

Webb smiled a thin little smile. "Yes, sir. In that case, we've got nothing right now. Rüdel's gone. He has a couple of guys with him, a little more than a ton of explosives, and no known associates or agenda. He's a ghost."

"O'Reilly, can you lean on your CI for more information?" Holliday asked.

"I don't think he has any more," she said. "He suspects Rüdel was working for Thomas J. O'Malley, but doesn't think that arrangement is still in effect. He's got no idea where Rüdel is, or what he intends to do."

"Okay, look into the O'Malley connection," Holliday said. "Lieutenant, do you need anything from me? More men? Resources?"

"I'll let you know, sir," Webb said.

"Unlimited overtime is approved until this case is closed," Holliday said. "I'll give you top-cover with the brass and I'll stay out of your way. All I'm asking is that you get him."

"Understood, sir," Webb said.

"Go to it."

Chapter 10

"Thomas John O'Malley," Kira read off her computer screen. She'd gotten a head start on the question when she'd started researching the O'Malleys the previous day. "Age 46, Caucasian male. Born right here in New York. Known associate of Evan O'Malley."

"Son?" Vic guessed.

"Nephew," Kira corrected. "He's got a record: couple of assault beefs, weapons, disorderly conduct, all from his younger days. Hasn't been on the radar the last few years. Runs a construction company, Emerald Isle Estates."

"Money-laundering front?" Erin asked.

"Not necessarily," Webb said. "The mob do whatever makes them money. It's probably a legitimate company, at least on the surface."

"They're just more flexible in what they're willing to do in their contract negotiations," Vic said.

"Why was he employing Rüdel?" Webb asked Erin.

"To take out Morton Carlyle."

"Why was he down on Carlyle?" Vic asked. "Besides the obvious."

"What the hell is that supposed to mean?"

"I was referring to the fact that Carlyle's a terrorist."

Erin's family had strong Irish Republican sympathies. "He's not a terrorist," she snapped. "The IRA aren't terrorists."

"No," Vic retorted. "They're just guys who blow up buildings for political purposes. What's the right word for that? Oh, yeah... terrorists."

"Knock it off, both of you," Webb said. "And somebody answer the question. Why would O'Malley want to whack Carlyle?"

"They're both mid-level lieutenants in the family," Kira said, consulting her spreadsheets and org charts. "They've got similar responsibilities, from what I can tell. The O'Malleys are better organized than most Irish mobs."

"Hey," Erin said.

"No offense," Kira said. "But they don't tend to be as firmly hierarchical as the Italian Mafia families. Anyway, the O'Malleys are split up by areas of business." She stood up and went to the whiteboard. Picking up a marker, she started diagramming.

"At the top, we've got Evan O'Malley. Par for the course, he never actually does anything illegal himself. He's got a son, Richard, and a nephew, our guy Tommy. Richard's a playboy, doesn't seem to be directly connected. Tommy and Carlyle handle the family's cash flow, as far as I can tell. Money laundering, with some gambling on the side. They keep their hands pretty clean. The big money-makers for the O'Malleys are construction and transportation on the quasi-legal side and drugs, prostitution, and gambling as straight-up crime."

"By 'transportation' I assume you mean smuggling?" Webb asked.

"Yes and no," Kira said. "They apparently get more money through legitimate shipping contracts than smuggling. They're plugged into the New York Teamsters. The guy who handles that is James Corcoran." Kira managed not to look at Erin as she added Corky's name to the board. "Drugs and women come through these channels..."

"Jones," Webb interrupted.

Kira pulled up short, her marker making an aimless black squiggle on the whiteboard.

"We're not the Organized Crime Task Force," he said. "I don't care about bringing down the O'Malleys right now. I care about stopping a possible terrorist. Now, I'm going to ask my question for the third time this morning. Why Carlyle?"

"Well, if you look at the chart," Kira said, a little miffed, "you'll see it branches out under Evan O'Malley. There's no second-in-command."

"The son would be next in line," Vic said. "Right?"

Kira shook her head. "The son's kind of a loser. Erin can double-check this with her contacts, but he doesn't seem like he's got much street cred."

"The nephew, then," Vic said.

"That's my point," Kira said. "I'm sure Tommy Jay would *like* to be next in line when the old man steps down or gets killed or whatever."

"But he's worried Carlyle is gonna get the nod," Erin said, getting it. "He was trying to take out his rival for the number two spot."

"Can he do that?" Vic asked.

Everyone looked at him.

"He's a mobster," Webb said, sounding like Vic had just said the dumbest thing he'd heard in a week.

"I know that," Vic said. "But Carlyle's a made guy in the organization. Tommy Jay would have to get permission from his uncle to take Carlyle out."

"Which is why he brought in Rüdel to do it for him," Erin said.

"Deniability," Kira agreed. "If Carlyle was taken out by an outsider, it wouldn't blow back on Tommy Jay, unless someone found out."

"Okay," Webb said. "But that doesn't help us unless Tommy Jay has information on Rüdel."

"How'd Rüdel survive his dip in the river?" Vic asked. "He had to have somewhere to lay up while he recovered. A construction company must have plenty of good locations."

"We need to talk to this guy," Webb said. "One of you has to stay here and hold the fort."

"I'll stay," Kira said. "I want to keep doing research."

"Okay," Webb said. "The rest of you, saddle up. Let's go see what Tommy Jay knows."

*　　*　　*

The corporate headquarters of Emerald Isle Estates occupied the entire eighteenth floor of a downtown Manhattan office building, a tower of glass and steel. On the elevator ride up, Vic looked at his reflection in the window.

"Should've worn my good tie," he muttered.

"Wouldn't have helped," Erin said. "You're a lost cause."

"Yeah," Vic said. "I probably lowered their property values just walking into the lobby."

The elevator glided smoothly to a stop and opened its doors onto a spacious reception area done in emerald green with gold trim and dark brown marble flooring.

"They're doing well for themselves," Webb said.

"You have any idea how much it costs to rent a whole floor of a downtown building?" Vic said into Erin's ear.

"I dunno," she said, playing dumb. "Couple thousand a month?"

The receptionist, a breathtaking brunette, gave them an incandescent smile. "Welcome to Emerald Isle Estates," she said with a hint of Irish brogue. "How may I be of assistance?"

"We're here to talk to Mr. O'Malley," Webb said.

"Do you have an appointment, sir?"

He flashed his shield. "Lieutenant Webb, NYPD. I think he'll be willing to take some time out of his schedule."

Her smile never flinched or faltered, Erin had to give her credit for that. "I'll ring his office. Just a moment, please."

Vic thrust his hands into his pockets and studied the gold Celtic knotwork that lined the countertop. "This stuff mean anything?" he asked Erin.

"My great-grandfather came over from Ireland," she said with a shrug. "I'm as American as you are. I don't speak Gaelic."

He shrugged. "I speak Russian. I figured maybe."

The receptionist was on her phone. "Yes, Mr. O'Malley," she said. "There's a Lieutenant Webb here from the police. I'm sorry, sir. Yes, sir. Yes, sir, they'll be right in. Thank you, sir." She hung up and turned her brilliant smile back on Webb. "Tricia will be out in just a moment to direct you to Mr. O'Malley's office."

"Thank you, ma'am," Webb said.

Tricia was another very attractive young woman. She escorted them down a hallway, then took a left and led them to a corner office. THOMAS J. O'MALLEY was emblazoned on the door in big, gold block letters. Tricia knocked lightly.

"Come in," a man said from the other side of the door. Tricia opened it and directed the detectives to go in. Once the three police officers and one K-9 had entered, Tricia stood in the doorway.

"That'll be all, Trish," said the man behind the desk. Erin heard the door close behind her.

Thomas O'Malley stood up. He was a big man, broad-shouldered and muscular, losing his middle-aged battle with his waistline. He gave the cops a once-over and smiled broadly. It was a pleasant expression that went no deeper than his lips. "What can I do for you, Lieutenant?" he asked, aiming the question at Webb. "Does your station need remodeling or maybe replacement? We've done several of the NYPD's precinct houses. The one-twelve down in Queens just last year. And then, of course, there was the renovation of the Civic Center, including your very own Police Headquarters."

"We're not here about a construction job, Mr. O'Malley," Webb said. "We just need to ask you a few questions about a business associate."

"Please, it's Tommy Jay," he said. He spread his hands. "Anything I can do to help. Can I pour you a drink?"

"We're on duty," Webb said.

"That's a rough life you lead," Tommy Jay said. "Rules like that, I'm surprised there's so many Irish on the force."

"We get the sober ones," Webb said, deadpan. "Now, Mr. O'Malley, if you can answer just one question, we'll be on our way and out of yours."

"Fire away, Lieutenant. Or can I call you Harry?"

"Where's Hans Rüdel?" Webb said.

Tommy Jay blinked. Then, with an exaggerated, comical gesture, he bent and looked under his desk. He straightened again with an expression of wide-eyed confusion. "I'm sorry, Harry. I don't see him anywhere. I can ask around the office, but I'm pretty sure I'd know if he were here."

Vic's eyes narrowed. Erin heard a low growl rumbling in his chest.

"Wrong answer," Webb said. He was still speaking lightly, almost pleasantly. "I guess we won't be leaving after all."

"Grand," Tommy Jay said. He indicated a pair of office chairs facing his desk. "Let's make ourselves more comfortable. I can have Tricia bring in another chair."

"I'll stand," Vic said. The other two detectives made no move toward the seats.

"Well, then," Tommy Jay said. "If you don't mind." He plopped back into his own chair, leaned back, and laced his fingers across his belly. "Now, all joking aside, I don't have the slightest idea where this Mr. Rüdel is, whoever he is. Why would you think I did?"

"We have information connecting you to him," Webb said. "You hired him to take out Morton Carlyle."

"I run a construction company, not an escort service, Harry," Tommy Jay said.

Vic muffled a laugh, turning it into a cough.

Webb wasn't laughing. "You sheltered him while he was recovering from his gunshot wounds," he said. "Where?"

"Harry, where do you get such wild ideas?" Tommy Jay asked. "Erin, Victor, you don't share his suspicions, do you?"

"I share all suspicions, all the time," Vic said. "On general principles."

"I'm suspicious of your knowledge of us," Erin said. They hadn't given him their names.

"I read about you in the papers, Detective O'Reilly," he said. "Hero of New York."

"You want to be a hero too, Mr. O'Malley?" Erin asked. "You want to help us, and help this city?"

"Every little boy wants to be a hero," he said. "Then he turns into a man and becomes more practical. They tell him crime doesn't pay, but they don't tell him heroism pays worse."

"You'd rather be a criminal than a hero?" she asked.

He shrugged. "Heroes are reactive. They only show up when something's already gone wrong. Businessmen build things. Men like me build this city; women like you just keep it from falling down. But I've never claimed to be a hero."

"You're going to be hearing from the Feds, Mr. O'Malley," Webb said. "Homeland Security isn't as understanding as we are."

"That's a shame, because I've always had a soft spot for the NYPD," Tommy Jay said. "But I can't give you what I don't have."

"Just so we're clear," Webb said. "If you have information on Rüdel's whereabouts or plans, tell us now. If you do, that's the end of it. If you don't, you're aiding and abetting a terrorist. And you know how we feel about that in New York."

Tommy Jay rubbed his chin in mock thoughtfulness. "I suppose if that's the case, I might as well swear off Catholicism, join Hamas, and bomb Israel. At least then there'll be no confusion. You won't have to bother with those pesky civil rights you claim to protect, either."

Erin briefly considered reaching across the desk and showing Tommy Jay what a civil-rights violation looked like up close. She settled for giving him the flat, hard stare she reserved for wiseass perps.

"Thank you for your time, Mr. O'Malley," Webb said. "If you do happen to think of something that's slipped your mind, or if you find out something we ought to know..."

"I'll give you a call," he said with his broad, insincere smile. "But from what you've been saying, you have important police business. I don't want to keep you from it."

"Give him a card," Webb said, signaling to Erin.

She obediently slid one of her cards onto his desk.

Tricia was waiting in the hall outside. She escorted them back to the elevators.

"You appealed to his civic duty?" Vic burst out the second the doors slid shut. "I don't believe this! While we're out chasing that happy asshole Rüdel, Tommy-boy will just sit back and wait for his construction contract to rebuild whatever the hell Rüdel takes out."

"That's a good point," Webb said thoughtfully. "An extra incentive for him not to help us. I hadn't thought of that. It'll help us make a conspiracy case against O'Malley, but only if Rüdel succeeds."

"Why hasn't he already succeeded?" Erin asked suddenly.

"What do you mean?" Vic asked.

"Why isn't there already a smoking crater in the middle of downtown? What's he waiting for?"

"It could be two things," Webb said. "Either he's not ready yet, or he's waiting for a specific time or event. Either way, the clock's running."

Vic shook his head. "Every time someone says that, I get an image of one of those timers they put on bombs in the movies. You know, with those little red numbers?"

"They don't use those in real life," Erin said.

"Why not?" Vic wondered. "If we ever end up next to a bomb, it'd give us something to watch while we're waiting to blow up."

"I've been next to a bomb," Erin said. "Believe me, it holds your attention. And speaking of time, that was a big, fat waste of it."

"Why?" Webb asked.

"He didn't give us anything."

"He's our guy," Webb said. "He hired Rüdel."

"How the hell could you know that?" Vic demanded.

"He claimed not to know who Rüdel was," Erin said.

"Exactly," Webb said. "If the name was Johnson or Smith, then maybe it would play. But Hans Rüdel has been all over the news. You'd have to have your head under a pretty big rock to miss it. And he reads the news; he knew the two of you, didn't he? If he knew who we were, he knows who Rüdel is. O'Malley talks too much."

"Great," Vic said. "Now there's just that one thing we need."

"Proof?" Erin guessed.

"Proof," Webb sighed.

"It really would be easier if they just let us throw assholes in jail," Vic said.

"Yeah," Webb said. "And we could rip the Constitution out of the National Archives and throw it in with them, so they'd have something to read."

"Can we get a court order?" Erin asked. "For Emerald Isle's construction projects?"

"Not with what we have," Webb said. "But the public buildings they worked on are a matter of public record. That's where we'll start."

Chapter 11

"I know why Siobhan Finneran's in New York," Kira said by way of greeting.

"I missed you, too," Vic said.

"You want me to pretend to be glad to see you, you pay up front, just like with your other girls," Kira said.

Vic's cheek twitched. "Say that again," he said.

"Why's Siobhan in town?" Erin said, stepping in front of Vic.

"I don't think she was lying about being on a business trip," Kira said. "She just wasn't forthcoming about what her business was."

"No riddles," Webb said. "And no more bullshit, any of you. We haven't got time."

"Scotland Yard sent over some info," Kira said. "Vic, did you ask for it?"

"I asked for everything they had on Evan O'Malley," he said stiffly.

"Siobhan's working for him," she said.

Erin wasn't surprised. It fit with Siobhan turning up at Carlyle's place. The only thing she hadn't expected was for

Carlyle to have covered it up, to have lied to her. She needed to talk to him again, and soon. "What line of work?" she asked.

"Contracts."

"She's an assassin?" Webb said, startled.

"Never proven," Kira said. "But they think she's done at least three killings in Northern Ireland, all mob-related. The Brits say she's a master pistol marksman. Er, markswoman? And a bombmaker."

"So she's working with Rüdel?" Vic suggested.

"I don't think so," Erin said. "I think she came here to kill him. And I know where to find her."

"She's peripheral," Webb said. "We find Rüdel, we don't need her. She'll just go back to Ireland once we've got the German locked up."

"So we just let a hit woman run around Manhattan?" Vic demanded.

"Unless and until she commits a crime on US soil, that's exactly what we have to do," Webb snapped. "Keep your head in the game. We're trying to stop a terrorist."

"Glad to hear it," a new voice said.

The detectives looked to the stairwell. Three men in black suits stood there, the two in the back wearing sunglasses. Erin thought they looked just like the bad guys from *The Matrix*. The leader stepped into the room and smiled pleasantly, which spoiled the effect.

"Agent Johnson, Homeland Security," he said.

"Agent Johnson," Webb echoed.

Johnson shrugged almost sheepishly. "I know, I've heard all the jokes. But that's really my name. Paul Johnson. Don't worry, I'm not here to step on anyone's toes. We all root for the home team." He came forward and extended his hand.

Webb shook warily. Johnson then shook hands with the rest of the squad. When he got to Erin, he glanced down at Rolf.

"Is your K-9 trained in explosives detection?"

"Yeah," she said. "Tracking and apprehension, too."

"That's good," he said. "Now, we've got quite a problem here. I understand there's a foreign national with a history of violence, military training, and a large quantity of explosives somewhere in Manhattan?"

"Before we get into that, I'm going to need to see some credentials," Webb said. Johnson's friendliness hadn't disarmed him.

"Of course," Johnson said. "Smith, please."

The guy on Johnson's right opened his briefcase and produced some papers that he handed to Webb. All three of the agents then opened their wallets in unison and showed their IDs. Webb scanned the documents.

"Okay, looks to be in order," he said grudgingly. "Welcome to New York."

"I was born here," Johnson said, confirming what Erin had already recognized in his accent. "Brooklyn. So as long as we're protecting turf, it's my turf, too. I've read Hans Rüdel's file. What's the status of the investigation?"

"Detective Neshenko will bring you up to speed," Webb said.

"What? Sir, I—" Vic began.

"He's very experienced at inter-agency cooperation," Webb said smoothly. "He's our liaison to foreign law-enforcement services."

Vic gave his lieutenant a look that promised payback, but squared his shoulders and walked over to the whiteboard. "Okay, guys, have a look here..." he began.

"That wasn't very nice, sir," Kira said in an undertone.

"Privileges of rank," Webb said quietly. "Shit rolls downhill. Now, Jones, I need you to look up the contract history of Emerald Isles Estates. See what public facilities they've worked on over the past, say, three years. Focus on current projects, or ones they've recently completed. I'll need job histories, blueprints, everything you can get."

"On it," Kira said.

"I have something to run down," Erin said.

"Is it going to leave us alone with the Feds?" Webb asked.

"Um, yes," she admitted.

"I figured. What've you got?"

"I saw Siobhan Finneran," Erin said.

"What?" he exclaimed. "When?"

The Homeland Security guys spun around, startled.

"It's nothing," Webb assured them. "Carry on." He turned back to Erin.

"Last night," she said.

"Where?"

There wasn't any way around it. "The Barley Corner."

Kira sucked in her breath through her teeth in a sharp hiss.

"What were you doing there?" Webb asked.

"Trying to track down O'Malley leads. She showed up out of nowhere. I don't think Carlyle was expecting her."

"She's working with Carlyle," Webb said in a soft, flat voice.

"I'm not sure," Erin said.

"Get sure," he said.

"That's what I want to do," she said.

"Okay, go. Now. I'll handle the Feds."

As Erin went down the stairs, Rolf by her side, her phone buzzed to indicate a text. She glanced at it and saw it was from Kira. It was just three letters long and read, "WTF?"

She thought for a second about what she could say that wouldn't compromise one or both of them. Then she tapped out, "I know what I'm doing."

By the time she'd reached the parking garage and was halfway to her car, she had Kira's answer.

"Like hell you do."

* * *

The lunch rush hadn't quite hit the Corner yet. A few guys were scattered around the place, but Erin didn't pay any attention to them. She angled straight for Carlyle at the bar.

He saw her and started to get up. "Erin," he began.

She put her hand up, index finger pointed between his eyes like a gun barrel. "Don't," she snapped. "Don't even start."

He had his back to the bar. She was pinning him in place, getting right in his face. Their eyes were less than six inches apart. "You son of a bitch," she said. "I actually believed you."

"I need to talk to you," he said quietly. "Thank you for coming."

The mildness of his reply threw her for a second, but she coasted on her anger. "You're not gonna weasel out of this," she said. "I want to know about Siobhan, right now!"

He raised one of his own hands past her, making some sort of gesture. She glanced to the side and saw Caleb and another big Irishman halfway to the bar. Carlyle was waving them off. Rolf had seen them too, and hadn't liked what he saw. He stood his ground at his partner's back, bristling.

"Not here," Carlyle said in an undertone. "If you'd care to step upstairs?"

"Like hell," she growled.

"As you please. There's a room down the back hall."

Erin realized he was right. They probably shouldn't thrash the whole thing out in front of whatever mob guys were there, plus anyone else who might wander in. She ground her teeth and stepped back far enough for him to move away from the bar. He reflexively straightened the lapels of his jacket and extended his arm toward the back of the building.

The back room had a green baize card table and a collection of leather-upholstered chairs. Carlyle motioned her to take a seat.

She wasn't having any of it. "Siobhan Finneran," she said. "I know what she is."

Carlyle sighed and sank into one of the chairs. The room was dimly lit by a green-shaded lamp over the table. It cast his face in half shadow. He looked very tired. "I'm ashamed to ask it, Erin," he said. "But I need your help."

She blinked. "Are you even listening to me? Damn it, you're working with an assassin!"

He shook his head. "I'm not working with her, Erin. It's not so simple."

"Seems pretty simple to me. Tommy Jay hires Rüdel to take you out, you bring in Siobhan to take care of him. You planning to have her whack both of them, or just Rüdel?"

"I didn't know she'd be coming, Erin. Word of God, I didn't."

"But you knew what she was."

"She's a frightened lass who lost her father and lost her way!"

"She's an assassin for the Irish mob!"

"I didn't want this," Carlyle said. "I don't want this. Not for her."

"But she came here," she pressed. "You had to know."

"Evan didn't tell me," he said. "Erin, you have to believe me."

This was the first time he'd ever said anything like that to her, sounding like an innocent man overwhelmed by events. She leaned forward, planting a hand on the tabletop, and looked in his eyes. She saw nothing in them but plain sincerity.

"You said you want my help," she said.

"I said I needed it."

"What do you need, then?"

He put his hand on hers. "I need you to stop her."

"What? Why?" Now she was really confused.

"You're a copper, Erin," he said and managed a slight smile for the first time in the conversation. "You need a reason to uphold the law?"

"You want me to arrest her?"

"I want you to stop her. Get to Rüdel before she does. Save her."

"You think Rüdel's going to kill her?"

"I think she's going to kill him." Carlyle sighed again. "Siobhan's a very talented lass, as I've told you. She took a great deal of interest in the activities of the Brigades, from her earliest years. I've not seen anyone with a more natural knack for firearms, nor a keener instinct for hunting. If he's still in New York, she'll find him, and when she does, she'll more than likely be the one who walks away. I don't want that on her soul."

"Jesus Christ," Erin said. "You're worried about her *soul?*"

"I'm worried that a lass I love will do something foolish and waste her life," he said. "I know the road I'm on, Erin. I don't want her walking it. I know exactly how it ends."

"Is she still here?"

"In the Corner? Nay. She left bright and early."

"You look pretty tired," she said, watching his eyes. "Neither of you got much sleep, did you?"

She saw a flash of anger, though his face remained outwardly calm. "She's like a daughter to me, Erin."

"Does she think of you as a father?" she retorted. "Or something else? Seems to me she's a little possessive of you."

"Why does that concern you?" he shot back. "She's nothing of the sort, but if she was my lover, would that bother you?"

Erin scowled at him. It *did* bother her, but that wasn't the point. "What did you two talk about after I left?" she asked more quietly.

"She wanted to know about you," he said. "Why you were here."

"Makes sense," Erin said. "We'd arrested her. That didn't give her much reason to like me."

"It was no easy thing to explain," Carlyle said. "I could hardly tell the lass why you were really there. She might have gone straight to Evan. But the best alternate explanation wouldn't do, either."

"Which was?"

He managed another slight smile. "Why else might a lad and a lass be sharing cocktails in the wee hours of the morning?"

"Oh, God," Erin said.

"Just so. I told her I was acquiring information from a law-enforcement officer. I may have implied the two of us had business dealings from time to time. It satisfied her, I think."

"Oh, great. Fantastic." Erin rubbed the back of her neck. "As if I didn't have enough problems."

"Erin, no one who knows you would believe that for a second," he said.

"You'd be surprised," she shot back.

Carlyle's face froze. He stared at her for a long moment. "Good Lord," he said at last. "You're under investigation?"

"What does it matter?"

He stood up. "You should leave," he said. "Now."

"Why? My boss knows I'm here. And I'm clean. You know that as well as I do."

"That's not the point," Carlyle said. "Damn it, lass, have you learned nothing at all? No one cares about the truth. They only care what a thing looks like. I'll not be the cause of your troubles."

"The hell do you care?"

"Because I do."

"How can I trust you? Hell, how can you trust me?"

"Doesn't matter how," he said. "But I do." His eyes showed nothing but earnest truth.

"When I got here, I was thinking of arresting you as an accessory."

A more genuine smile crossed his face. "That doesn't surprise me."

"And it doesn't bother you?"

"You'd do it because it's your job," he said. "If you did it because you wanted to, that might bother me."

"I *did* want to."

"Do you now?"

She thought about it. She sighed. "No."

"Then we've naught to worry ourselves over," he said. "But now we need to plan, darling. You know about Tommy Jay, aye?"

"We know he hired Rüdel," she said. "But we can't prove it yet."

"The proof doesn't matter," he said. "What matters is you're looking in the right place."

"Vic damn near killed Rüdel," she said. "He put two rifle rounds through him. We think Rüdel was laid up for a couple months, hiding out and recovering. Makes sense that Tommy Jay would've hidden him."

"Aye," Carlyle said. "Probably at one of his work sites."

"And maybe he's still there," she said. "But we can't get a warrant for their company records with what we've got."

"You don't need a warrant," he said. "I can get them for you."

"Really?"

"I know a lad."

For the first time since getting there, Erin smiled. "Okay, do it."

"And you need to be more careful," Carlyle said. "You don't want to be guarding your back from your own lads. Believe me, I know."

"I can handle them."

"Erin," he said, then paused.

"What?"

"I shouldn't say this," he said. "If anyone finds out you heard this from me, I'm likely a dead man."

She waited, letting him work through it.

"We've a lad in your precinct," he said. "It's no snipe hunt your lads are on."

She felt a chill. "Who?"

"I don't know. He's not one of mine. You're my only contact within the department at present, and as you said, you're clean."

"Then whose is he?"

"Tommy Jay's," Carlyle said. "He'll not tell any of us how he gets it, but he knows things only a lad with an ear in the police could hear. You understand, I can't ask about this within the Family."

"Right," she said. "Especially if we scoop him up down the line. Do you know it's a guy, not a girl?"

"Nay, that's only a guess."

"Figures. Let me know when you get your hands on the Emerald Isles records."

"I'll see you get them."

"How do you do it?" she asked.

"Do what?"

"I came in here spitting nails. Now... Christ, I feel like I should be thanking you."

"You know how to thank me."

Erin blinked at him, wondering what he was implying. Then she remembered his request, to stop Siobhan. "I'll see what I can do."

She had her hand on the doorknob when he said, "And Erin?"

"What?"

"You're a fine copper."

"And you're a first-class gangster."

"I'll take that as a compliment."

"As a matter of fact," she added, "you're the best gangster I've ever met."

"Including Corky?"

She wrinkled her nose. "Definitely."

Chapter 12

"Give me good news, O'Reilly," Webb said.

She'd had a chance to think about what to say, but she still wasn't sure. The meeting with Carlyle hadn't gone at all the way she'd expected. It wasn't that she didn't know what she was supposed to do. She was supposed to report everything.

But Carlyle was right. Things weren't simple.

"Carlyle didn't hire Siobhan," she said. "The O'Malleys aren't working with Rüdel, either. They want to find him as bad as we do."

"Why do they care?" Vic wondered.

"Probably because they know if some damn terrorist blows up a building in Manhattan, and gets linked to them, we're gonna come down on them like a ton of bricks," Webb said. "Okay, O'Reilly. So what's Finneran's game, if she's not taking orders from Carlyle?"

There it was. The question she wasn't sure how to answer. "Carlyle doesn't have anything to do with her work," she said. Even as she said it, she realized she sounded just like him. "But I think we'd better find Rüdel before she does, for everyone's sake."

"For her sake at least," Vic said. "If I have to choose between a bulletproof former-military neo-Nazi and a hot Irish redhead, I know who I'd back in a fight."

Erin thought about what Carlyle had said about Siobhan's natural talent. "Maybe," she said. She directed Rolf to his usual spot beside her desk. The Shepherd flopped down and rested his head on his paws.

Agent Johnson had been on the far side of the room. Now he walked over to join the conversation. "Excuse me. You've had a fair amount of contact with the Irish, is that right?"

Erin raised her eyebrows. "You could say that. *I'm* Irish."

He laughed. "Right, of course. I meant, the Irish Mafia."

"No one calls it that," she said. "Both sides would be offended by the comparison."

"The O'Malleys," he said. "You know what makes them tick?"

It was her turn to laugh. "It's not complicated. They'd say they're businessmen first, criminals second. It's all about the money."

"Okay," he said. "Where's the money for them in this? If we offered, say, half a million dollars for Hans Rüdel, would they deliver him?"

"You're serious?"

He grinned. "It worked on Bin Laden."

"Navy SEALs got Bin Laden."

"With intel from guys who wanted the reward."

"So we're the Navy SEALs in this comparison?"

Johnson laughed again. "I suppose. But do you think it would work?"

She thought it over. "No," she said, thinking of what Carlyle had said about the truth. "These guys care about appearances. If it looks like they're working for the police, they'll get taken out by their own people. And in any case, I don't think they know where he is."

"It was worth a try," Johnson said. "Well, let me know if you have any bright ideas. At this point, we might settle for anything that's not completely crazy."

Erin felt like she might be going a little crazy herself. She needed a minute or two to collect her thoughts. She decided to go to that classic refuge, the ladies' room.

The moment she was inside, she realized she'd made a tactical error. She'd momentarily forgotten that one of the people she wanted to escape from was also female.

"God damn it, Erin!" Kira hissed, pushing the door shut behind her and leaning against it. "Are we on the same team or not?"

"We are!"

"So what's going on here?" Kira demanded. "What am I missing? We agreed it was a bad idea for you to be getting that close to the O'Malleys, so what do you do? Run over there, by yourself, in the middle of the night!"

"I used to break curfew in high school, too," Erin said.

Kira didn't laugh, or even crack a smile. "This is serious!"

"You think I don't know that?" Erin shot back. "I'm doing everything I can to catch a crazy bastard. If I have to use Carlyle and the O'Malleys, I will."

"You're using them? You sure it's not the other way around?"

"Everyone uses everyone," she shot back. "That's how the world works. Just ask Lieutenant Keane!"

"I don't have anything on the O'Malley mole," Kira said. "Hell, it'd take a major IAB investigation to pry open something like this. We don't have the resources and we don't have the time. We're not gonna find this guy before Internal Affairs burns you. I want to help you, Erin, but you're not making it easy."

"And what are you doing?" Erin retorted. "I'm following the trail. All you're telling me is what not to do. You gonna help me here, or just hold me back?"

Kira's jaw went rigid and for a second Erin thought the other woman might actually take a swing at her. Then Kira's muscles relaxed. When she spoke, Erin still heard the anger in her voice, but it was quiet and resigned.

"If that's the way you feel, Erin, I'm not going to get in your way. But I'm sure as hell not going down with you, either."

Kira opened the door and left. As it swung shut, Erin heard Vic making an old joke about women going to the restroom in pairs. Erin went to the sink and splashed water on her face. Her cheeks were burning. The cool liquid felt good.

"Okay," she muttered. "I guess I'm on my own, then."

* * *

Erin couldn't handle being in the Major Crimes office right then. She could feel Kira very deliberately not looking at her. The tension was driving her crazy. There wasn't anything to do but wait, anyway. She'd only sat at her desk for a few minutes when she stood up again.

"Where you going?" Vic asked.

"Downstairs," she said. "To the range."

"I'll come with you," he offered, starting to get out of his chair.

"No thanks," she said. She wanted to be alone.

"Whatever," Vic said, sinking back into place.

"Keep your phone on you," Webb said. "We may need to move fast."

"Rolf, *hier*," she ordered. He obediently trotted out of the office at her heels.

Down on the range, she got a box of nine-millimeter bullets, her ear protection, and a set of headphones for Rolf. He looked ridiculous, but dogs had sensitive hearing and it was important to protect them. She could've left him upstairs, but it was good for him to be around gunfire every so often, to make sure he stayed calm when bullets started flying for real.

She set up a target at the short edge of intermediate range; fifteen yards. Starting with her Glock holstered, she squared off, drew, and fired twice, aiming for center mass, following up with an aimed shot at the head. Then she reholstered her gun and did it again. And again. She fell into the practice rhythm. Draw, double-tap to the chest, one to the head. It was called the Mozambique Drill, and was the recommended technique for quickly dropping an enemy at close range.

Shooting was a kind of meditation for Erin. She imagined herself firing thoughts out of her brain like bullets, emptying her mind. She emptied a clip, reloaded, and did it again. Eventually, calmness and a little clarity returned.

There were just too many problems. She had a cop-killing terrorist to catch, an Internal Affairs investigation to avoid, an Irish hit-woman to stop, and a dirty cop to nail. And it was all tangled up together, so she kept trying to see the whole picture at once. What she needed to do was bite off one piece at a time. The question was, what could she deal with first?

Erin needed advice. The one person in her life she could always count on for that was her dad. Unfortunately, if her phone really was being tapped, she couldn't talk openly with him.

At least, not on her own phone.

Erin stepped away from the range, broke down her gun, and cleaned it. Then she called her sister-in-law.

"Hey, Shelley?"

"Erin!" Michelle said, and in spite of everything that was happening, Erin smiled. Her brother's wife was always genuinely happy to talk to her. She was the closest thing to a sister Erin had, and was one of the kindest, most positive people she'd ever known.

"When are you coming over?" Michelle asked. "You haven't been by in a while. Anna misses Rolf."

The conversation was going exactly the way Erin wanted it to. "Actually, I was thinking of dropping by after work," she said. "You don't need to put on anything special, I can just—"

"Nonsense," Michelle said. "You work full time, I'm a housewife. Besides, I've already got chicken and dumplings going in the Crock Pot. If your mom taught me anything, it's never to let a guest go hungry. Especially family."

Erin laughed. "Okay. But I might get held up at work. If I'm late, go ahead and start without me."

"We're used to unpredictable schedules," Michelle said. "Your brother's called me from the hospital more times than I can count. That's the good of the slow cooker. We'll aim for six-thirty, but it's flexible."

"See you," Erin said and hung up. Then there was nothing left to do but go back upstairs and back to the grind.

* * *

The afternoon was full of the sort of boring police work civilians didn't think about. They were trying to narrow down Rüdel's location on the basis of sketchy information. Kira kept plotting possible sightings on her map. All of them spent a lot of time on the phone, talking to witnesses, informants, and Patrol officers. None of it did any good.

"It's crazy," Vic muttered. "That guy who blew up the Olympics in Atlanta disappeared for years, but he was hiding in the backwoods. This bastard's in New York City."

"There's plenty of places to hide in the city," Webb said. "You just have to know the ground."

"But Rüdel doesn't," Vic retorted. "He's a foreigner. Someone's hiding him."

"Doesn't help us," Webb said. "Unless we know who."

"We do," Vic said. "Thomas O'Malley."

"And we can't move on him without a court order," Webb reminded him.

"Let me see what I can do," Agent Johnson said. "We have a different set of rules."

The Homeland Security guys disappeared to make some phone calls. And Erin went to see her brother's family.

*   *   *

Sean O'Reilly Junior lived in a brownstone on Manhattan's Upper West Side, the sort of neighborhood Erin knew she'd never inhabit, not on a police salary. But Sean was a trauma surgeon and Michelle came from money. Erin would've felt out of place there if the O'Reilly residence didn't feel so much like a home. But her family was there, and that made all the difference.

"Aunt Erin! Rolfie!" her niece Anna exclaimed as she opened the door. The eight-year-old threw her arms around Rolf's neck. Rolf, badass police dog that he was, took the embrace with patient dignity. He let Anna pull him inside and bury her hands in his fur.

Michelle came to the kitchen door, drying her hands on a dishtowel. "Hey, sis," she said. "Come on in. Dinner's about ready. Sean won't be joining us, I'm afraid. I just got a call from him. There was a three-car pileup in the Lincoln Tunnel. He'll probably be at the hospital all evening."

"Sorry to hear it," Erin said. "Could you remind me what my brother looks like?"

Michelle laughed. "Sometimes I need the reminder, too. But I knew he was a doctor when I married him."

They sat down to a delicious home-cooked meal. Erin reminded Anna not to pass food to Rolf under the table. Patrick, Michelle and Sean's other kid, had started kindergarten that fall, but he was going through a shy stage and didn't want to talk about it. Erin, watching Michelle trying to draw the boy out, thought there were some similarities between motherhood and police work. Maybe she could get Shelley a job as an interrogator if she ever got tired of being a housewife.

Anna needed no interrogation. She was going to be a policewoman, just like Erin. And a doctor, just like her dad. And she'd volunteer at the Humane Society on the weekends, helping find homes for puppies.

"I thought you were going to be a ballerina," Erin said.

"That, too," Anna said cheerfully. "But I think dance will be more of a hobby."

Erin nodded soberly. "Sounds like you're gonna be busy."

"I like doing stuff," Anna said. "You're looking for the guy who shot that cop. Did you find him yet?"

Michelle gave Erin a mortified look. "She picks things up from the news," she explained.

"It's okay," Erin said. "No, we haven't found him yet, Anna. But we're still looking."

"You'll catch him," Anna said with a child's careless certainty. "Then you'll put him in jail."

"That's the idea," Erin said.

"Can't Rolfie follow him? With his nose?"

"Rolf's nose is very good," Erin said. "But if a bad guy gets in a car, or a train, then he can't tell where the guy went."

"When I can't find something," Anna said, "Mommy says to look in the last place I left it."

"It's not always that easy, kiddo," Erin said.

After dinner, Erin went into the kitchen with Michelle to help clean up, while Anna and Patrick played with Rolf in the living room. Once the dishwasher was loaded, Erin said, "Shelley? Can I ask a favor?"

"Sure. What's up?"

"I need to call Dad, but I can't use my phone. Can I borrow yours?"

"Of course." Michelle looked at her. "Dead battery?"

"Technical issues," Erin said. She didn't like to lie to her family, and that was almost the truth.

"Okay, you can use the one in the master bedroom."

"Thanks." Erin started for the stairs.

"Erin?" Michelle called.

She paused in the doorway. "Yeah?"

"Is everything okay?"

Erin was afraid of what might be written on her face. "You could've been a cop, you know that?" she replied. "You've got great instincts."

Michelle laughed and shook her head. "Not a chance. I don't have the stomach for it. Seriously, you all right?"

"Forget about it. It's just police stuff."

"If there's anything we can do..."

"I know. Thanks, sis." Erin went upstairs and, after a moment's hesitation, closed the bedroom door. She punched her parents' number into the bedside phone, thinking how strange it was to use a telephone with an actual physical cord and buttons.

"O'Reilly," her dad answered.

"Hey, Dad."

"Hey, kiddo. You good?"

"About that..."

"Trouble?" Sean O'Reilly asked sharply.

"I could use some advice, Dad."

"About life, or the Job?" That was the word old cops always used about policing. She could hear the capital letter.

"The Job."

"Glad I can still teach the hotshot detective a thing or two," he said. "What's up?"

"I remember something you told me a while ago," she said. "Back in the '90s, you had a partner that got in some trouble. Nate."

"Yeah," he said cautiously. "I remember."

"He was taking payoffs," Erin said. "From the Mafia?"

"Yeah," he said again. She could tell he wanted to ask her what was going on. His worry was obvious, even over a crappy phone connection from upstate New York.

"You had Internal Affairs breathing down your neck," she said. "Until Morton Carlyle gave you the IA file on your partner. You agreed to testify." She took a deep breath. "What if he hadn't given it to you? What would you have done then?"

Sean didn't answer right away. She waited, giving him time.

"I don't know," he said at last. "I guess it comes down to a choice."

"Between what?"

"Betraying someone else or betraying yourself."

"Was he your friend?"

"No. He was my partner. That's more than a friend, you know that. A friend won't necessarily take a bullet for you. Erin, is one of the guys on your squad into something?"

"There's a mob mole somewhere in the Eightball," she said.

"How do you know?"

"I got a tipoff. IA is looking at... they're looking at *me*, Dad."

"Oh, Christ, Erin," he said, and she knew exactly what look was on his face. It was the one he'd had when she'd broken one of her mom's favorite dishes when she was a little girl. The look that said Erin O'Reilly had really stepped in the shit. "What have you gotten into?"

"Dad," she said. "I'm still me. I'm not into any of that. But what if I can find out who is?"

"You working IA now?"

"No! But if they come after me, what can I do?"

"Cooperate," Sean said wearily. "Tell them what you know. But you don't want to get a rep as a snitch."

Erin sighed. "So, cooperate, but don't tell them anything that matters? Thanks, Dad."

"It's not an easy spot to be in. The main thing is, you need to do what's right. That's how we raised you. You know the right thing to do here?"

"Yeah. I guess I do."

"Then what are you asking me for?"

She couldn't help smiling at that. "No idea."

"Sergeant Malcolm still working the desk?"

"Yeah," she said, wondering about the sudden change in subject.

"Say hello to him for me."

"I will."

"Us old cops, we don't know much, but we do know a few things."

"Thanks, Dad."

"Be careful."

Chapter 13

Erin went home frustrated. She knew Michelle heard it in her voice when she excused herself, but she was too pissed off to hide it. She didn't know what she'd been hoping to get from her conversation with her dad, but she hadn't gotten it.

"You know," Michelle said at the door, "you can talk to me if there's something..."

"Thanks," Erin said, a little shortly. She knew she wouldn't take her sister-in-law up on the offer. Michelle was a wonderful person to talk to, but she was a civilian. She wasn't going to drag her into this.

When she got back to her apartment, the first thing she did was unclip her shield and gun from her belt. The second thing she did was pour herself a stiff double whiskey. Then she fed Rolf, slumped down on her couch, and turned off her brain.

She opened her eyes and sat up abruptly. The room was dark. She must have fallen asleep. Rubbing her eyes, she looked at the clock. Quarter past nine. She hung on to the thought that had woken her and pulled out her phone, dialing the precinct's desk number. Then she waited on hold for ten minutes. That was what she got for calling the non-emergency line.

"NYPD, Precinct 8," the answer finally came.

"Detective O'Reilly," she said, thinking she recognized the voice on the line. "Is this Malcolm?"

"Yeah," he said. "It's kind of crazy here, kid. What's up?"

"Sarge, do you know if Lieutenant Webb's still up in Major Crimes?"

"Nah, he left a couple hours ago. You need him for something?"

"No, that's okay. There was something I had to take care of. I may drop by for a little."

"We could use you. Thinking of coming back to Patrol, doing some real work?"

"I should do that, kick the rest of you lazy bastards into shape."

"I'd like to see you try it." He paused, and she heard a commotion in the background. "Damn. Have to go. Drunken assholes, you know how it is."

"Sure thing, Sarge."

Erin hung up and got off the couch. Her Glock and shield went back on her belt. Rolf jumped to his feet, tail wagging, ready to go back to work.

"Easy, boy," she said. "Sure, you can come. But we're gonna be coming right back. This'll be quick."

Rolf's tail didn't stop moving. He was still on board with the plan.

*   *   *

Middle evening was a quiet time in some occupations. Not policing a major city. Erin stepped into the usual semi-organized chaos of a busy precinct house. Arrests were being processed. Complainants were hanging around the desk, filling out forms, waiting to talk to officers, and giving unsolicited and profane advice about how to run the department. Erin didn't mind. She'd worked Patrol for eleven years. This sort of thing felt like home.

She didn't go upstairs. She hadn't really come to visit Major Crimes. She'd come to see Sergeant Malcolm.

The thought that had struck her was that her dad hadn't been acting normal. Sean O'Reilly was a born straight shooter, honest as they came. His awkward shift at the end of their conversation had been a message, from a guy who wasn't used to talking in code. He wasn't asking after an old friend; he was feeding her a tip.

It was just a hunch, but at this point, Erin was ready to give hunches a try. So she hung around the desk, waiting for a quiet moment to talk to Malcolm.

She waited a while. Malcolm was efficient, but he also had a lot to do. While she loitered, Erin thought about how to approach him. She didn't know whether her dad thought Malcolm knew something about dirty cops, was dirty himself, or had some other information. In fact, she didn't even know whether Sean had really given her a message. So she had to be careful.

He noticed her hanging around, making intermittent eye contact across the room, but there was no opportunity to even say hello until there was a gap in the precinct traffic. Her chance came at ten, when Malcolm went to grab a coffee break and had a patrolman sit in for him. She snagged him when he stepped out from behind the desk.

"Hey," she said, intercepting him on his way to the first-floor break room.

"Hey, kid," he said. "What's up now?"

"You're not drinking that shit, are you? Come on up to second and I'll get you a cup of the real stuff."

"You Major Crimes types and your fancy new coffee machine."

"That's right." She grinned. "It's because we're extra-special."

"As in, special education?"

"That's not very PC."

"I'm too old to worry about that." Malcolm was a thirty-year man. "Sure, I'll take a cup. Maybe it'll make me smart, handsome, and successful."

"More than you already are?"

"Hardly seems possible." He smiled.

Major Crimes was quiet, as Erin had guessed. The Homeland Security agents had gone wherever they went when they weren't protecting democracy, and her fellow detectives were nowhere in sight. But Holliday's light was on under his office door. More importantly, the espresso machine was still turned on. Erin poured two cups and handed one to Malcolm. He added two lumps of sugar and a packet of creamer, took a sip, and sighed contentedly.

"Oh, that's fantastic," he said. "You're a lifesaver."

"How's it going down there?"

"Typical weeknight."

"That bad, huh?"

"No one's thrown up on me yet, so it's better than some."

Erin wrinkled her nose. "Yeah, that's one thing I don't miss about Patrol."

"You telling me they never puke on you here?"

"Not yet," she said, trying to think how to get at the reason she was there without tipping him off.

"How's your old man?" he asked

"He's good. He likes being retired. You should try it sometime."

"You know what they say?" Malcolm asked, taking another sip. "The guys who do their twenty and collect their pensions, they do fine. Become security consultants, shit like that. But the guys who stay in till mandatory kicks in? A year or two, tops, and boom! They're gone. Heart attacks, car crashes, hell, suicide."

"You telling me you're staying in the Job because you think it'll kill you to retire?" she asked, only half joking.

He shrugged. "Stats don't lie, kid."

That was the sort of thing Kira would say. The thought hurt Erin more than she'd expected. "Maybe they need to feel useful," she said. Bending down, she scratched Rolf behind the ears. "K-9s are like that. They don't take retirement well."

"There's worse ways to leave the Job," Malcolm said. "Death and disability come to mind."

"Like Hendricks," Erin said.

Malcolm shook his head. "Yeah. Poor kid. Shitty luck."

"Yeah," Erin said, taking a drink of her own coffee.

"He wasn't even supposed to be in that PSA," Malcolm said, meaning Public Service Area.

"What do you mean?"

"I saw the tour assignments," Malcolm said gloomily. "Hendricks and Michaelson subbed for Polikowski and Worth."

"Someone get sick or hurt?"

"Nah. Michaelson asked for that assignment."

"No shit," Erin said. No wonder Michaelson was beating himself up over it. "Guys swap PSAs often in the Eightball?"

"It happens. Usually it's no big deal."

"Unless someone gets hurt," she agreed.

"You guys any closer to catching the bastard?"

"We're still looking," she said. "We don't know where he's going, or how he got there. All we know is where he's been."

"Better than nothing," Malcolm said.

"Not much," Erin said. But she suddenly remembered what her niece had said about looking for missing things. Maybe Anna had been onto something.

"Look, I gotta get back on the desk," Malcolm said. "Thanks for the drink. Hey, is it true, what they say?"

"About what?"

"Your coffee machine."

"What are they saying?"

"That it was a gift from a mob guy."

Erin didn't have the slightest idea how to answer that, so she just replied, "What do you think?"

He laughed. "That'd really be something. Take it easy, kid. Leave some glory for the rest of us. And say hi to Sean when you see him. We used to have a grand old time down in Queens, back in the day."

*   *   *

Erin watched Sergeant Malcolm go back downstairs and wondered what the point of the conversation had been. Maybe her dad was wrong, and Malcolm didn't know anything. Or she hadn't asked the right questions. Or maybe she'd been expecting too much from an overworked desk sergeant.

She rubbed her temples and stared at the Major Crimes whiteboard, looking for inspiration. But Anna's words kept running back through her head. *When I can't find something, Mommy says to look in the last place I left it.*

It was a silly idea, of course. Rüdel wasn't a pair of scissors or a spare sock. But maybe going back over the ground where he'd been would shake something loose. And it wasn't like she had any better ideas.

She didn't bother calling in. Rüdel would hardly be returning to the scene of the shooting. She'd just walk the area again, then go home and maybe get some sleep. Erin bundled Rolf into the Charger and drove to the warehouse.

Abandoned crime scenes were just about the saddest, most depressing sights in the world. After the bodies were carted away, all that was left was just empty space, bloodstains, police tape, and dark memories.

Erin and Rolf stood on the pavement outside the warehouse. A single streetlight cast their shadows across the street. The K-9 waited patiently, watching her. She stared at the darkened building, thinking.

They'd been so focused on what had been taken, and on the shooting. When a criminal escaped from the scene in a place like Manhattan, if they didn't catch him right away, there wasn't much point following where he'd gone. There were just too many people, too many places to hide. And Rüdel was too canny not to have a good escape route lined up.

She knew she was looking at things wrong. Or she was looking at the wrong things. She walked to the warehouse door and tried to put herself in Rüdel's place. He hadn't gone there to kill a cop; his plan had been to go in, grab some explosives, and get out. He and his guys came outside, saw the police car, shot Hendricks, and pinned Michaelson down. Then they ran around the corner and out of sight. Michaelson didn't pursue. He was outnumbered, outgunned, and trying to save Hendricks.

Erin walked Rolf around the corner. What she saw was what had been there the last time she'd looked; an ordinary stretch of New York City street. The shooters had jumped into the car they'd had waiting, then driven away.

No, that wasn't right. If they'd been loading a car, why not park right outside the warehouse? They could have used a panel van. It wouldn't have attracted any attention. In fact, it would have screened the door from view, so they might not have needed to gun down a policeman in the first place.

But if they hadn't had a car, that was just plain crazy. Carrying several hundred pounds of stolen explosives by hand? Erin shook her head.

"Military training," she muttered. Rüdel was a former soldier, and grunts understood the importance of transportation and logistics. She slowly scanned the street again, looking for what she'd missed.

Just a few feet in front of her was a storm sewer manhole. The lid was slightly ajar.

Erin looked at the manhole and weighed the possibilities. As she thought about it, the idea made more sense.

"That's how they disappeared," she said to Rolf. "No one saw them. And once they were down there, they could go just about anywhere." The honeycomb of tunnels under New York City was legendary.

She knelt by the manhole and took hold of the edge. The lid was cast iron and weighed a ton. Erin strained and shifted it, scraping metal against blacktop. Then she sat back and took a deep breath. A musty, rusty smell wafted into her nostrils.

Erin knew it was time to report. She pulled her phone and fired off a quick text to Webb: *At shooting site. Think R went through the sewer. Looking for evidence.*

She wasn't about to wait for more cops to show up and hold her hand, though. Rüdel would be long gone. This was just to see if she could find some trace of the perps' passage. If she could figure out at least the direction they'd gone, then might be the time for CSU. She'd just take a quick look around, see what she could find.

Erin went back to her car and buckled on her vest. She also got Rolf's, just in case, and suited him up. The dog presented an issue. She wasn't sure he could handle the rungs of the ladder on his own, and she wasn't going down there without him. So she fished out a coil of nylon rope from the trunk. She passed it through the harness loops on Rolf's vest. He stood patiently while she got him ready. He'd been trained for rope descent from a helicopter, and this was about the same. Erin lowered him into the hole, foot by foot, until a splash told her he'd hit bottom. Then she followed him down.

It was only when she reached the bottom and splashed into knee-deep, ice-cold water that an uncomfortable thought struck Erin.

The manhole cover had been shut tight the last time she'd been at the crime scene.

Someone else had come down that ladder since then. And that someone might still be in the sewer with them.

Chapter 14

The heavy D-cell flashlight felt comforting in Erin's hand. She shone the beam in a slow circle, taking in the storm sewer. She and Rolf were in a long, low tunnel. It was one of the older sewers in Manhattan. A roof of red brick arched above an artificial underground river. The water was almost up to her knees. Rolf was belly-deep in the stuff, and she knew it would take more than one bath to get the smell out of his fur.

She had two directions to choose from. Would Rüdel have gone toward the East River, or upstream?

"Rolf, *such*," she said.

Most people assumed a dog couldn't track through water. While it was true water could carry scents away, it was also true that smells lingered in the air above it. If the quarry had passed recently enough, a good dog could track them. And Rolf was very good.

The Shepherd didn't know who he was supposed to follow, so he cast about for the strongest, most recent scent in the tunnel. He turned to his right, tail wagging, and splashed toward the subterranean heart of Manhattan.

Erin knew she should call in an update, let Webb know where she was going. Rolf's leash was in one hand, her flashlight in the other. She shifted the light to her opposite hand and fumbled out her phone. There was no signal. That wasn't surprising. She was insulated from the cell towers by twenty feet of brick, dirt, blacktop, and concrete. She put it back in her pocket.

All kinds of crazy shit floated around her and protruded from the floor of the tunnel. Plastic bottles, soda cans, discarded shirts and shoes. She recognized the metal cage of an overturned shopping cart. Erin and Rolf had been vaccinated against most urban diseases. They probably wouldn't get sick from anything down here.

Something bulky and metal loomed in front of them. She blinked. Was that a *refrigerator?* The tunnel was wide, there was plenty of room to go around it, but she had no idea how it had gotten down there. Rolf gave it a cursory sniff, then ignored it and kept going.

While they waded through water and urban litter, Erin was thinking. Rüdel's crew must have brought a boat, probably an inflatable motorboat, and used it to move their cargo. It was a clever idea, and it gave them the freedom to move a big pile of explosives almost anywhere under the city. Knowing that didn't tell her where they'd gone, though.

Rolf was excited. Being underground didn't bother him a bit, and he had a good scent to follow. He pulled Erin as quickly as she'd let him. They took a right turn, then a left, then another left. Erin tried to remember the exact route. Getting lost down here wouldn't be any fun. If she did get turned around, probably the best thing to do would be to find the nearest surface access and get topside, rather than try to retrace her steps.

Rolf paused an instant, then angled hard right, making for a gap in the brickwork. Erin saw that someone had broken a hole in the wall of the storm sewer. A jagged-edged doorway, just big enough for a large man, loomed in front of them.

She switched her flashlight to her leash hand again and played its beam into the opening. She unholstered her Glock with her other hand, holding the gun alongside her hip. She saw dust and old concrete support pillars, but no sign of life. Taking a deep breath, then wishing she hadn't, she sloshed out of the sewer.

Erin found herself in an abandoned subbasement. It was scattered with trash, but not as dirty as it should have been. It was the sort of place New York's homeless should have found irresistible. The walls were bare of graffiti. No vagrants lurked in the corners. The litter looked to be twenty years old, at the least.

Rolf snuffled at something to one side of the doorway. Abruptly, he sat perfectly still, staring at it. That was his "alert" posture for explosive detection. Erin turned to see what he'd found.

Her heart jumped into her throat. She was staring at a curved rectangle of olive-green plastic, about the width of a sheet of paper, positioned on a small tripod. The words FRONT TOWARD ENEMY were looking her right in the face. She was staring at a Claymore antipersonnel mine. It was a nasty little piece of military hardware, a layer of C4 explosive backing a few hundred steel balls. When one of those went off, it was like the biggest shotgun in the world. It would shred anything in front of it.

"Holy shit," she breathed, thinking back on the basic demolitions training she'd gotten when she'd been partnered with Rolf. A Claymore was usually manually detonated. She panned her flashlight beam all around the device and didn't see a firing wire. Afraid to move, she kept looking.

A slight reflection of something shiny caught her eye. She carefully bent her knees and looked closer. What she saw was a length of ordinary fishing line running from the mine across the doorway, less than an inch in front of Rolf's front paws. It was a tripwire trap.

"Holy shit," she whispered again. "Rolf, *bleib*."

Rolf obediently continued sitting.

Erin holstered her Glock and knelt beside the tripwire, setting her flashlight on the ground so its beam shone across the wire. It wasn't exactly safe to mess with a live explosive, but she wasn't about to leave a lethal trap down here either. She'd disarmed a bomb before. She reached into her pants pocket for her Swiss army knife and opened its little scissors. Moving very carefully, she closed one hand around the fishing line, holding it steady. She slipped the line between the blades of the scissors and slowly closed them.

The line parted easily. Erin let out the breath she'd been holding and looped back the loose end of the line. It was time to call in the backup. This was getting out of hand. She stowed her knife and got her phone out again. Just one bar of service, but it'd have to be enough.

"Stay still, *bitte*. Put down the telephone."

Erin froze. She didn't know the voice, but she had a pretty good guess who it was. It had come from behind one of the support columns in the subbasement.

"I'm a detective with the NYPD," she said, speaking slowly and clearly. "Identify yourself."

"*Ja*, I know you," the man said. "I remember you from the docks. You were with the big blond man. Did he die, when I shot him?"

"Hans Rüdel," Erin said. She considered her chances. If she moved out of the light quickly enough, she might be able to get her gun out. But not before taking fire. She remembered the incident he was talking about. Specifically, she remembered him planting two shots in Vic's center of mass. The range had been double what it was here. Maybe her vest would protect her. And maybe he'd go for a head shot this time. She glanced at Rolf. He was still sitting, as she'd ordered him, but he was staring into the darkness. His hackles rose slowly. If she released him, he'd go for Rüdel.

"*Ja*, you remember," Rüdel said, sounding pleased.

"Come on out, let's talk," she said.

"I think not. You are looking for me, *ja*? Why else are you here?"

"There's a lot of people looking for you. You'd better come in before they find you. You're better off with me than with them."

"The Irish?" Rüdel laughed. "O'Malley told you about me, then. Stupid *schwein*. I am doing this as much for him as for anyone."

"How's it going to help him?" Erin asked. She had no idea what he was talking about, but one of the tricks of interrogation was to pretend you already knew what the perp knew. A lot of mopes would spill if they thought they weren't giving anything away.

"In the end, of course, it will help your people, too. The *Polizei* will be stronger than before," Rüdel said. "That is the point. But there is a period, first, of adjustment. O'Malley will find opportunities there."

"You *want* a stronger police force?" Erin said. She carefully shifted her weight, bringing her feet under her, balancing herself for a quick lunge.

"Of course," Rüdel said. "You Americans. You all wring your hands because you think your police are too strong. But all your demonstrations, your riots, these show your police are not strong enough. I want to make your country stronger, safer. You do not understand me at all. I like America. I like Americans."

"Okay," Erin said. She had a pretty good fix on his position. He was behind the second column from the left, from the sound of it. If she could figure which side of it he was looking around, she could move to keep the pillar between them. That would buy enough time to get her gun out, even the odds. In the meantime, she wanted to keep him talking. "How are we gonna end up stronger, though? Shooting our guys doesn't help you there."

"You are wrong!" he exclaimed. "Killing is the only thing that will do the job! Crisis is all you Americans understand. You get so comfortable, so lazy. The World Trade Center, that got you on your feet. It was a good start."

Erin felt a chill. She'd known she was facing off against a dangerous man, a killer, but until that moment, she hadn't seriously considered the possibility that Rüdel might be totally insane. "You said you liked America," she said, trying to keep her voice steady. She remembered 9/11. The thing she remembered most about that day was wondering where her dad was, and hoping he'd come home alive at the end of his shift.

"I do," Rüdel insisted. "But it needs a, how do you say, a push in the right direction. The direction it should go. America for the Americans, the Anglos. Not any of the others. We make America stronger, and she fights our wars for us. Germany was wrong the last time, you see. We tried to take on the whole world, especially America. We never should have fought America. It was the Russians that were our true enemies. They are your enemies, too. We should be friends."

"Friends don't kill each other and blow up buildings," she said. She was trying not to look directly at him, but she was pretty sure he was on the left-hand side of the column.

"It is necessary," Rüdel said. "In any case, your politicians will blame the Arabs. They always do. That will be the convenient thing."

"You've really thought this through," Erin said. But the main thought in her mind was that, if Rüdel hoped to blame his plan on someone else, he couldn't very well explain it to Erin O'Reilly and then leave her alive. Her main goal in this conversation, she reminded herself, wasn't to find out his plan. Her main goal was to get out of this room still breathing.

"One of your politicians, Jefferson, said the tree of liberty had to be refreshed with blood," Rüdel continued. "But liberty does not come from war. You think too much of your liberty."

"So you're going to knock down the foundations of our freedoms?" Erin guessed, wondering what that meant in New York. Was the crazy bastard going to try to blow up the Statue of Liberty?

"*Nein!*" he retorted. "What good would that do? Your sentimental press would make her into a victim. The way to strengthen authority is by attacking it!"

Erin was having trouble following the thread of Rüdel's paranoid neo-Fascist crazy-talk, but she felt like she was getting closer to an answer. "The police," she said quietly.

"I like you," Rüdel said suddenly. "You will be good for this city, after."

She didn't find that particularly comforting, not with what he'd said he'd do to a place he claimed to like. "Look," she said. "There's other ways you can get what you want."

"I think not," Rüdel said. "Always, it comes back to violence. That is the only way anything ever changes. So now—"

Erin was getting ready to make her move, but she wasn't ready for what happened next. Neither was Rüdel.

A pistol cracked twice, above and behind Erin's head as she crouched on the concrete. In that confined underground space, the sound was tremendously loud. She'd been half-expecting a gunshot, but not from behind. But she'd been primed to move, so she did.

Erin rolled to her right, angling to force Rüdel to come out of cover after her. As she went, she saw a muzzle flash in the darkness ahead. Her foot clipped her flashlight. It spun across the room, leaving a trail of disjointed, strobe-light images blazed on her retinas. For just an instant, crazily, she thought she saw a female face. She saw a swirl of something that might have been a red ponytail. Two more muzzle flashes flared. A shower of concrete chips stung her cheek from a near miss. Then she was up on one knee, Glock in hand, looking for a target.

"Rolf!" she shouted. *"Fass!"*

At his "bite" command, the Shepherd lunged forward, snarling. Erin might not be able to see Rüdel, but Rolf's nose was harder to fool. Erin's ears were ringing from the close-range gunfire. She had no idea what was going on, who was where.

She didn't even know who'd fired the first shots. "Who's there?" she challenged. "NYPD!"

There was no answer. Either the newcomer wasn't a cop, or Rüdel had gotten them with his return fire.

She heard Rolf as the tinnitus in her ears started to subside. He was scratching at something and growling. That meant he couldn't get at his quarry, probably because of a every dog's worst enemy, a closed door.

Erin scrambled across the floor to her fallen flashlight and snatched it up. The lens was cracked, but the bulb still worked. She shone the beam in the direction she thought Rüdel had gone and saw Rolf on his hind legs, pawing at a steel door set in the far wall.

She spun around and played the light into the tunnel she'd come from, half-expecting a gunman to be standing there, or a dead body floating on the water. The passage was empty.

Erin wanted to go after Rüdel, run him down. But that was a terrible idea. She'd only barely escaped one booby trap. There were probably others. And he had a couple accomplices somewhere nearby. Plus, he was on his guard now. She scooped up her phone and dialed Dispatch.

No service.

"Damn, damn, damn," she muttered, trying it again. Still nothing.

There were times when a cop needed to back away from a situation. Erin didn't like it, but this was one of those times. She called Rolf. They needed to fetch the cavalry.

Chapter 15

To Webb's credit, he didn't waste time getting angry. The speed of his arrival was impressive. He and the rest of the squad were on scene less than fifteen minutes after Erin clawed her way, dripping wet, out of the nearest manhole and called in a 10-13. The "officer needs assistance" call guaranteed a rapid response from every available Patrol unit, and Manhattan had a very dense police presence. By the time Major Crimes got there, the place was already crawling with uniforms.

Erin was back underground when Webb found her. She hadn't been able to haul Rolf out, so she'd stayed topside only long enough to call for reinforcements. Then she'd gone back to her dog. Half a dozen cops had fanned out into the abandoned subbasement, but they hadn't tried to open the door Rüdel had gone through. After Erin showed them the Claymore mine, they decided to wait for the Bomb Squad.

"Start talking, O'Reilly," Webb said as he splashed out of the sewer tunnel, not bothering with preliminaries. Kira and Vic were right behind him.

"Rüdel's down here," Erin said.

"You sure?" Vic asked.

She glared at him. "Maybe it was some other neo-Nazi terrorist just hanging out in the sewers."

He held up his hands. "Hey, I gotta ask."

"There's another shooter down here, too," she said.

"Rüdel's got a gunman with him?" Webb asked.

"No, someone else," she said. "Someone trying to take out Rüdel. I'm pretty sure it was—"

"Finneran?" Webb interrupted.

"Yeah. I think I saw her."

"She tag him?" Webb asked.

Erin had been thinking about that. "I don't know," she admitted. "It happened fast, in the dark. Rüdel fired a few rounds, Siobhan shot two or three times. She might've clipped him, but if so, he wasn't hit bad. He moved fast and didn't leave a blood trail."

"Where's she now?" Vic asked.

Erin shrugged. "She took off. I needed to stick close to Rüdel's location, so I didn't follow."

"Damn," Webb muttered. "The last thing we need is the Irish fighting World War II under Manhattan all over again."

"Actually, the Irish were officially neutral in the Second World War," Kira said.

It was Webb's turn to glare.

"They even had Nazi sympathies," she went on. "Irish President DeValera was the only world leader to extend official condolences to Germany when Hitler died..." Her voice trailed off. "You don't care, do you."

"I really, really don't," Webb said.

"Why don't we just open the door?" Vic asked.

"You know what happens when one of those things goes off?" Erin replied, pointing to the Claymore where it still sat, small and menacing, beside the entrance.

"Makes sausage," Vic said. He didn't sound overly worried.

"*People* sausage," Kira said. "There's about seven hundred ball bearings in one of those."

"He's getting away," Vic fumed.

"He's gotten away," Webb corrected. "If he had an escape route laid on, he's already out of here. But we don't need to chase him if we know where he's going. Any ideas, team?"

"He's going to attack the police," Erin said.

"How do you know that?"

She quickly recounted her conversation with Rüdel.

"Wow," Vic said. "This guy is totally out of his gourd. We're talking Looney Tunes."

"I think his reasoning is pretty sound," Kira said. "After major terrorist incidents and external attacks, history shows people tend to lean toward more authoritarian regimes. It's a way of reclaiming a sense of security."

"Bullshit," Vic growled.

"Says the Russian," Kira said, giving him a sweet but insincere smile.

"I've got an idea," Webb said. "How about, instead of arguing whether the psycho has a point, we work on catching him before we have to find out if his plan works?"

"Who's a psycho?" a new voice said from behind them.

"Hey, Skip," Erin said.

Skip Taylor, Bomb Squad tech, climbed out of the sewer tunnel. "We gotta stop meeting like this, Erin," he said with a grin. "What is it this time?"

"Crazy neo-Nazi terrorist," she said. "With at least one Claymore mine."

"Awesome." Skip had already spotted the Claymore. He knelt down and looked at it. "This guy a pro?"

"Former military engineer."

"Good."

"Someone explain why that's good," Vic said.

"He's using military hardware, with military training," Skip said. Then he casually picked up the antipersonnel mine and tossed it into the air.

The air pressure in the room dropped from all the sudden intakes of breath.

Skip caught the explosive one-handed. "It's good for three reasons."

"Should I be taking notes?" Vic snorted.

The tech ignored him. "One, it means the hardware's reliable. It won't go off unless it's supposed to. Two, it makes him predictable, and I can predict him; because three, I've got some of the same training he does. I know what kind of traps he's likely to set."

Skip was an EOD expert who'd done time in Iraq. He was used to people trying to blow him up. He walked across the room to the door Rüdel had gone through. He lay down flat on the concrete, ignoring the thick layer of dust and dirt. Pulling a narrow-beam flashlight off his belt, he shone it through the thin gap at the bottom of the door. Then he reached into his bag for a fiberscope and threaded it into the gap. He sat up and stared at the device's screen, steering the head of the artificial snake to take in everything on the far side of the door.

"Well?" Webb demanded.

"I had a CO back in the sandbox who always wanted us to rush," Skip said. "It was always now, now, now with him. Right up until I found five IEDs in the house he wanted for his command post. You rush your case, sir, a perp walks. I rush my job, maybe nobody walks out of here. So, with all due respect, sir, if you'd let me concentrate on my fucking job, sir, I'd appreciate it."

Webb looked like he wanted to strangle Skip, but he shut up and stood back. Vic grinned and said nothing.

Skip stood up. "Glad you didn't open the door," he announced.

"What've we got?" Webb asked. "If you're finished with your observations, that is."

"Tin can trap."

"Cans on a string?" Erin asked. She was thinking of a homemade noisemaker.

"Sort of," Skip said. "It's old-school. Viet Cong used 'em in Nam. Tie a tripwire to a grenade, pull the pin, stick the grenade in an empty tin can. The wire's across the door. You open the door, the wire pulls the grenade out of the can, the lever comes off the grenade, the fuse arms, and a few seconds later, bang."

"Jesus," Webb muttered.

"It's no big deal," Skip said. "You want it out of the way?"

"As soon as possible."

"That an order, sir?"

Webb rolled his eyes. "Yes, it's a goddamn order." He turned away.

"Yes, sir," Skip said, dropping back to his stomach and taking out a length of wire bent into a hook on one end. He slipped it under the door.

"Crazy bastard veterans," Webb said. "They think just because they've been in a war—"

A tremendous bang made the door tremble on its hinges. A cloud of dust, dislodged from the ceiling, showered down. Three of the uniformed cops dove for the floor.

Skip hopped up. "It's disarmed, sir."

Webb gritted his teeth. "That's not what disarmed means where I come from. You set the damn thing off!"

"With a steel-core door between it and us," Skip shrugged. "A frag grenade can't penetrate that sort of barrier."

"You could've warned us."

"Is the way clear now?" Erin asked.

"Roger that," Skip said.

"Then why are we still standing here talking?" Vic demanded. "Let's go get the son of a bitch."

"Carefully," Kira said. "There may be more booby traps."

"That's what he wants you to think," Skip agreed. "Classic combat-engineer mentality. They say, if an engineer wants to get you by the balls, he will."

"Good thing I don't have any," Erin said. She opened the door.

She saw a dark, dusty concrete hallway. Rusty pipes hung overhead. A blackened area of concrete was just inside the door. Little chunks of jagged metal peppered the door, walls, and pipes. She tried not to think about what would have happened if she'd gone through right away instead of calling for help.

Rüdel's path was clear enough. His footprints were plain in the dust, with the prints of other feet around them; his accomplices, most likely. More cops were close behind her. But not too close. They'd been a little spooked by the grenade.

They proceeded carefully down the hallway, Rolf and Erin in the lead. Rolf's nose brought them to a maintenance hatch, which led to a back corridor full of spare parts for some sort of machinery. That in turn brought them through another old brick wall with a hole knocked in it. The cops emerged into a dark, tubular tunnel lined with two sets of rusted, parallel rails.

"Old subway," Webb observed.

"This place is a goddamn maze," Vic said.

"That won't stop Rolf," Erin said.

There were a lot of myths about a dog's tracking ability. Erin had heard them all, and they were mostly bullshit. You couldn't escape by crossing running water, or by wearing somebody else's shoes. Spreading pepper in your footsteps might slow Rolf down, but only until he got to the far side and picked up the trail again. Even burying yourself six feet under wouldn't stop him. He'd dig with his own paws until the guys with the shovels showed up.

Unfortunately, he had limits, and they ran into one less than a quarter mile down the tunnel. The disused subway joined onto an active track. Rüdel's trail led straight to the nearest platform. Rolf scrambled up onto the concrete, Erin and the others close behind, guns in hand. They found themselves face-to-face with a handful of bemused civilians who were waiting for the next train.

"Nassau Street," Vic read, looking at the sign on the wall. "Shit."

Rolf had lost the trail, which meant Rüdel had gotten on a train. And that meant he might be at any other station on the route.

"Brown line," Kira said. "Northbound."

"Where's that lead?" Webb asked. He was a transplant from Los Angeles and didn't have a native New Yorker's knack for the subway.

"Past City Hall, through Chinatown, Little Italy, and the Lower East Side before it takes the Williamsburg Bridge over to Long Island," Kira said without bothering to look at the map.

"So he could be anywhere in southern Manhattan," Webb sighed. "If he's in Manhattan at all. God damn it."

"The stations have security cams," Erin said.

"That's worth checking," Webb said. "Jones, get on the horn. I want the footage from every station on the line. Neshenko, O'Reilly, take three units with you and start checking the stops. See if the dog can pick up anything. I'm going back to the Eightball to liaise with Homeland Security and get us some more bodies."

"This is gonna take forever," Vic muttered.

"C'mon," Erin said. "What else were you gonna do tonight?"

"I dunno. Sleep?"

"You wanted to sleep, you should've been a florist like your parents wanted."

"I never should've told you that."

"Relax. I'm sure you'd have been the manliest florist in the five boroughs. Very thorny roses."

"Go piss on the third rail, O'Reilly."

*   *   *

It was as bad as Vic expected. They got on a northbound train with half a dozen Patrol officers, then hopped on and off at every single station. Rolf had Rüdel's scent, as clear as if he had a photograph of the guy in front of his nose, but they had to check the whole length of each platform. The Shepherd caught a scent at the Canal Street station. Rüdel headed west, but only as far as the southbound Green line, where his scent disappeared again.

"Jesus," Vic swore. "He's yanking us around."

"Yeah," Erin agreed. "But we'll find him."

But they didn't. Rolf didn't pick up the smell again. They went all the way south to Bowling Green, at the southern tip of Manhattan, with no luck.

"You think he went to Brooklyn?" Vic wondered.

Erin rubbed her eyes. It was going on three in the morning. She'd been on duty for what felt like about a week. The adrenaline rush from the gunfight in the basement was a distant memory. "How the hell do I know?" she retorted.

"Maybe your dog missed something," one of the uniforms offered.

"The hell he did," she shot back.

"Where is this asshole, then?" the Patrol cop asked.

"Either he rode the train to the end of the line," Vic said, "or he got off somewhere along the way."

"How long it take you to come up with those options?" Erin asked.

He glared at her. "I mean, he could've pulled the emergency stop and gotten out in the tunnel. Or he could've used the back door on the train at one of the stations, gone straight onto the tracks."

"So what do we do?" another uniform asked.

"Sit tight," Erin said. "I'll call it in, find out what the LT wants."

Webb didn't sound happy with Erin's news, but he didn't sound surprised, either. "This guy's slipperier than Dick Nixon," he said.

"Nixon got caught, sir," Erin pointed out.

"And we haven't caught Rüdel yet," he replied. "How're you feeling?"

So tired I could sleep where I stand, she thought. "I'm good to go," she said.

"And your dog?"

Rolf was watching her. He definitely looked droopy. If he'd had a clear trail to follow, he'd have gone on until he dropped, but drawing so many blanks was hurting his morale.

"He'll go on if I do," she said.

Webb wasn't buying it. "You've done what you can for now," he said. "I talked to Agent Johnson. We've got a bunch of feds and NYPD all over the subway lines. We're gonna do blanket coverage. You and Neshenko go home, grab some sleep. We'll need you rested tomorrow. Today. Whatever."

"We can still help," she protested, but it was halfhearted and they both knew it.

"Come on back," Webb said. "We've got a busy couple of days ahead. We'll need to keep searching, and even if we catch him, don't forget the department funeral."

"For Hendricks," she said. It was crazy, but she really had forgotten it.

"Yeah. Day after tomorrow, two o' clock," Webb said. "After the Commissioner's press conference at One PP at noon. He's going to be doing his best to reassure the citizens of our fair city, while he talks about what a great job the NYPD is doing. I want him to be able to say Rüdel's in custody, and for that, I need my detectives sharp. So get your rest. That's a direct order."

Chapter 16

One of the worst feelings Erin knew was being too tired to stand, but too wired to sleep. The adrenaline had worn off, but she kept seeing snapshots of memory: the tripwire in front of Rolf's paws, the muzzle flashes of handguns in the dark, the swirl of red hair and the lightning-quick glimpse of Siobhan's face. She was more sure than ever that she'd seen the Irishwoman under the city. Not that the knowledge did her any good. She'd already known Siobhan was hunting Rüdel. The thought struck her, not for the first time, that if the assassin got to him, it would solve an awful lot of problems.

Erin turned over in her bed and stared at the clock on her nightstand. The glowing red digital numbers read 4:03. She raised her head and looked at the foot of the bed. Rolf lay curled in a ball, his snout tucked under his tail. At least one of them was going to be rested.

She wanted to sleep, needed it. But she was still trying to figure things out. Where was Rüdel? What was he going to do?

She'd stay awake until she knew her next move, she decided. Just a few minutes longer. Something would come to her.

Her phone was ringing.

For a moment, stupid with sleep, she didn't recognize the sound. Then she fumbled for the phone. It fell off the nightstand, bounced off the floor, and landed under the bed.

How long had she been out? Like any cop used to working nights, she'd installed thick, heavy curtains that didn't let in any light. Her clock now read 8:47, and she didn't know whether that was morning or night.

Mumbling a curse, she rolled out of bed and lunged for the phone. It was on at least its fourth ring. She grabbed it and swiped the screen.

"O'Reilly," she said.

"Is this line secure?"

"I—what?"

"I apologize for waking you. You needn't say anything. Take a moment, gather your thoughts."

Carlyle. She silently thanked him for his caution. IAB might still be tapping her phone. "I'm just getting up," she said. "Sorry. I had a late night."

"I know you're busy, so I'll not keep you long," he said. "But I've something you might be interested to see."

"I need to head in to work," she said. "I was thinking of grabbing breakfast on the way at the Sunrise Bakery."

"Then I'll not keep you," he said. "Perhaps we'll run into one another later. Until then, darling."

He hung up.

*   *   *

"I'll admit, I wasn't certain you'd come," Carlyle said fifteen minutes later.

"This cloak-and-dagger shit is new to me," Erin said between bites of croissant.

They were at a corner table at the Sunrise Bakery, just down the street from the Barley Corner. Erin had thrown on her clothes and hustled out the door with Rolf. She still felt half-asleep, unkempt, and confused. Carlyle, across the table, was as perfectly put-together as always. She'd only seen him disheveled once, and it had taken a bullet wound to do that.

"I apologize, darling," he said. "But I didn't wish to get you in greater difficulties with your superiors. I thought a bit of subterfuge might be excused under the circumstances."

She nodded. "Yeah, I get it."

He looked more closely at her. "Erin? Are you all right?"

She actually laughed at that. It came out shakier than she wanted. "I almost got killed a couple times last night. Oh, and I think your Irish girl might've saved my life by accident. So I'm just fine. Peachy. Forget about it. You said you had something for me. What is it?"

Carlyle's concern seemed genuine. Erin was normally irritated when men worried about her, but she found herself touched by his interest. It was more personal than business. That was something she couldn't deal with. Not with a terrorist trying to blow up a chunk of Manhattan. "Come on, Carlyle. Spill."

He sighed and hefted a briefcase onto the table. Unfastening its latches, he produced a thick manila envelope. "It's the projects Emerald Isles completed over the past three years," he said. "Bids, contracts, blueprints, the whole works."

She took the envelope but didn't open it. "How'd you get these?"

"Is that something you really want to know?"

"Can any of this be traced back to you?"

"I'd be grateful if you didn't mention how you acquired this information."

"I'll call it an anonymous tipoff, then. Thanks."

"My pleasure, Erin."

She finished her croissant in a last big bite and got up from the table. Carlyle stopped her with a hand laid across her own.

"You saw Siobhan?" he asked.

"Yeah."

"Be careful, Erin. Even though I told her..." he trailed off, uncharacteristically hesitant.

"What'd you tell her?"

"I told her you were important," he said. "And to make certain nothing happened to you."

Erin's brow furrowed. "Thanks," she said again.

"You'd best be off," he said, drawing back his hand. "Go save our fair city."

*   *   *

"What's this?" Webb asked.

"Emerald Isle's construction projects," Erin said, upending the envelope. Blueprints and paperwork cascaded onto Webb's desk.

"And these came from...?"

"Anonymous."

"Oh yes, our good friend Anonymous," Webb said, picked up the papers and beginning to sort through them. "Does it ever depress you just how many people don't want their good deeds coming out?"

"Maybe they're modest."

Vic snorted. "Maybe they're afraid their asshole friends will dump them in the Jersey swamps."

Erin gave him a look. "This guy's trying to help us."

"Doesn't do us much good," he retorted. "Rüdel's healed up now. He's not at any of these places." He picked up a handful of blueprints. "Hell, these are finished projects, most of them.

People live in 'em, work in 'em. I don't think Rüdel was ever in any of these. Look, we've got a community center, an apartment block, hell, they've even got the Civic Center. Hey, Lieutenant, did you know the Irish mob remodeled police headquarters? What a joke."

Erin felt a sudden chill. She was thinking of what Webb had said about Rüdel, when she'd asked why he hadn't already set off his bomb. Either he wasn't ready, or he was waiting. She reached for the blueprint Vic was holding. "You're right," she said.

"Huh?"

"This isn't about Rüdel hiding out. These are targets."

"What do you mean?" Vic asked.

She hoped she was wrong, but was afraid she wasn't. "He's a combat engineer, right? Everything he needs to target the weak point of one of these buildings is right here in these plans."

Webb was watching her with his eyes narrowed. "You know where he's going, don't you."

"And when," she said. She pulled the blueprint out of Vic's hand and put it down on Webb's desk.

"Oh, shit," Vic muttered.

They were staring at the plans for Number One Police Plaza, Manhattan Civic Center.

"The press conference," Erin said. "Tomorrow at noon."

"Attack the police," Webb said quietly. "Just like he said. When we're on the national news."

"There's no way," Vic said, shaking his head. "That place is secure. We're talking about the headquarters of the biggest police department in the country. Who is this guy, the goddamn Terminator? He's not gonna just walk in."

"We had a Rüdel sighting there," Kira said from behind her desk. She was the only detective who hadn't come over to look at Erin's folder. "It wasn't confirmed, but it still gives some support to Erin's theory."

Webb rubbed his forehead. "Just great," he said. "If we don't catch this scumbag, instead of declaring victory, the Commissioner's gonna have to give his speech with a bunch of ESU guys around him in full tactical gear. Yeah, that'll really make people feel secure."

"Cancel the conference," Erin suggested. "Or postpone it, at least."

"Even better," Webb said. "Here's the headline: 'NYPD Folds Under Threat From Lone Terrorist.' You seriously think the Commissioner will sign off on that?"

"So what do we do?" she demanded.

"You keep looking," he said. "I get on the phone with those jackasses at Homeland Security and we start talking about how to guard the building. That won't be detective work. It'll be uniforms, boots on the ground."

"You think that'll be enough to stop Rüdel?" Erin shot back.

"Yeah, I do," Webb snapped. "New York hasn't had a major terror attack since 9/11, and it's sure as hell not happening on my watch. Where the hell are those Homeland Security bastards, anyway?" He pulled out his phone and started dialing.

"You sure about this?" Vic asked Erin.

"I can't be sure until the building blows up," she said. "Or we catch him."

"I get him in my sights again, he's not walking away," Vic said, gritting his teeth.

"The ACLU ever hears you say that, the PC's gonna airmail you to Staten Island," Webb said. "You'll spend the rest of your life handing out parking tickets."

* * *

Agents Johnson and Smith were already en route to the precinct when they got Webb's call, and they were in Major Crimes less than five minutes later. They listened carefully as Webb laid out the situation and showed them the blueprints.

"This anonymous source," Johnson said. "Does he know when the attack's likely to go down?"

Webb glanced at Erin.

She shook her head. "He's not working with Rüdel and he's not in contact with him. This is..."

"Conjecture?" Agent Smith suggested.

"An educated guess," she said.

Smith looked at Johnson. "Conjecture."

Johnson sighed. "We can't shut down the Civic Center indefinitely, on suspicion," he said.

"No, we can't," Webb agreed. "The Commissioner will never go for it."

"What sort of fanatic is Rüdel?" Johnson asked. "Is he going to strap on a bomb vest and walk right into the lobby, or what?"

"He's a combat engineer," Vic said. "He'll plant charges."

"Where?" Smith asked.

"Jones," Webb said. "Would you call down to the Bomb Squad and see if Taylor's around? We could use him."

Skip was in the office almost before Kira hung up. They brought him up to speed.

"If he wants to bring down the building, he needs to hit the support columns," Skip said. "But he'd need a lot of explosives to manage it. And he'd need access to most of the building. I don't know how a wanted guy could do it. I mean, the place is crawling with cops. He wouldn't get five steps. So I'm guessing he's planning something else. Probably looking to cause mass casualties, like at the Boston Marathon."

"Can he pull it off?" Johnson asked.

Skip shrugged. "Of course. Especially if he's willing to die doing it. We'll need security checkpoints, sniffer dogs, the works. Get enough guys, the right guys, with training and experience... I'm guessing we could catch him. Maybe."

"Anything you need, you've got it," Johnson said.

"Talk to the Captain," Webb said. "He can coordinate with you Federal boys."

Erin didn't like it. The whole thing was way too reactive, waiting for Rüdel to make his move and hoping they were on the ball when he did. What if he hit a different target altogether? Or if their timing was off? But she didn't know what else they could do. Rüdel had gone to ground—or under it—and they had no way of knowing where.

They kept talking about security for the press conference. One PP was already a veritable fortress; they were just looking to fill in the gaps. The Homeland Security agents knew their work. Listening to them, Erin almost felt reassured. But she couldn't shake the thought that they were missing something important, that Rüdel was planning something they hadn't figured out.

Chapter 17

The whole day went to planning. A day wasted, in Erin's opinion. She worked late, trying to think what else they could do, but she had nothing. There'd be extra uniforms and plainclothes officers all over One PP, along with all the other potential targets from the Emerald Isles blueprints. Homeland Security had descended on Manhattan in force to back up the NYPD. Probably, Vic muttered darkly, they were running their own investigations without okaying it with the police. He didn't trust the Feds.

Erin almost wished she was a beat cop again, doing perimeter security. At least then she wouldn't have to pretend she had some say in what was going on. She and Rolf were sidelined. She stared at maps, building plans, and case files, and couldn't think of a damn thing.

At eight thirty Webb sent everyone on the squad home. "We've got the bases covered," he said. "Search teams are still down in the tunnels. They'll let us know if they've got anything, so keep your phones on you. But the detective part of this is on hold. Any of you think of anything, call me."

Tired, hungry, head aching, Erin led Rolf to the garage and loaded him into her Charger. She buckled her seat belt, started the engine, and then just sat there, staring at the steering wheel. She had no idea where to go. Home? What was the point? She wasn't about to sleep.

She thought of the Barley Corner. She'd skipped dinner, and the Corner had an Irish stew that reminded her of her mother's cooking. But that was crazy. Carlyle was already walking a dangerous line, feeding her information. To go right into his establishment might bring trouble.

On the other hand, she was a regular at the Corner. If she stopped going, that might also send signals, either to Internal Affairs or to the O'Malleys.

Irish stew sounded good, and if she was honest with herself, the thought of talking to Carlyle wasn't unpleasant. He was the one person who was helping her simply because he liked her. And maybe he'd have some insight. Besides, if the O'Malleys really did want Rüdel out of the way, what would they care if Carlyle was helping a cop take care of their problem?

"Yeah," she said to Rolf. "Maybe I am a little crazy."

She put the car in gear.

*   *   *

The Corner was full of mobsters. That might have just been Erin's prejudice talking, but eleven years as a cop had taught her to recognize these guys, and there were an awful lot of tattooed, muscular young guys at the side tables. They didn't look like they were there to have fun, either. Their conversations were pitched low, and they weren't paying much attention to anything else. She'd be willing to bet half the men in the bar were packing. The hairs on her neck stood up. She glanced down at Rolf. He was confident. He figured he could take anyone in the room.

Erin squared her shoulders and went straight to the bar.

"Evening, Erin," Danny said. "What can I get you?"

"Irish stew and a Guinness."

He grinned. "Coming right up." A few seconds later, he slid her drink across the bar.

"Erin, darling," Carlyle said. Just like that, he was there at her elbow.

"Evening," she said.

He leaned forward, resting his arms on the bar. Without looking at her, he said, "Do you think it's wise to be coming here, given the current situation?"

She shrugged. "What's the difference? If anyone's watching me, I'll make them suspicious whatever I do. So I'll do what I want."

He laughed and turned to face her. "Ah, now you're beginning to think like one of us!"

"Is that a compliment?"

"Do you want it to be?"

She took a sip of Guinness. "I'm not one of you, Cars."

"And I'm not one of you, darling. Yet you keep coming back."

Erin stared into her drink. "We lost him."

"Aye, so I've heard."

"Your girl hasn't found him, has she?"

"Not to my knowledge."

"We think we know what he's doing," she said.

Carlyle raised an eyebrow and said nothing.

"He's hitting police headquarters. Tomorrow."

"The press conference before the funeral," he said, getting it at once. "That's sensible, given his agenda. He'll want the world to see it."

"We've got guys everywhere," she said. "He's not getting into that building."

Carlyle nodded. "And you're certain that's his target?"

"No." She clenched her fist around the beer glass. "How can we know for sure?"

"According to Thomas O'Malley," Carlyle said quietly, "our friend Rüdel was already in possession of rather extreme views on the subjects of government and law enforcement. He believes Rüdel's near-fatal experience at the hands of your colleague this summer may have directed his energies in a specific manner. I fear he may be right."

"You've talked to Tommy Jay?"

"I talk to a great many people, Erin. At the moment I'm talking to you."

"And what do you tell people about me when they ask?"

He smiled gently. "Very little."

"Well, if he tries to hit One PP, we'll get him," she said with more confidence than she felt.

"Grand," Carlyle said. "Then tomorrow we'll celebrate his downfall together."

One of the waitresses appeared with a bowl of stew on a plate with a couple of dinner rolls. "Here you go, ma'am."

"Thanks, Caitlin," Erin said, recognizing her. She tore one of the rolls in half and dipped it in the stew.

Carlyle was thinking, drumming his fingers on the bar. "If he's looking to cause mass casualties, he needn't be inside the building," he said.

"Car bomb?" Erin guessed.

"Perhaps. But I think not. Since September 11, your lads have put all manner of obstacles around public buildings. A car couldn't get close enough to do serious damage to the facility. I suppose he might set off a device nearby, but that'd not be spectacular enough for the likes of him."

"So he can't bring down the building from the outside?"

"I didn't say that." Carlyle rubbed his chin. "I said I didn't think he'd use an automobile to deliver it. One needn't be inside a building to destroy it."

"Yeah, I guess you could drop a bomb on it."

"That's not precisely what I meant."

"Tell you what," She looked him square in the eye. "Tell me how Cars Carlyle would do it."

"You want me to plan the destruction of New York's Civic Center?"

"That's what I'm asking."

"And this isn't a particularly creative sting operation?"

That drew a startled laugh from her. "No!"

"Very well. I'll need to be thinking on this. I know you've little time. How late will you be awake tonight?"

"You think I'm sleeping?" Erin retorted. "Carlyle, for cops, sleep is like sex. We talk about it a lot more than we get it, and some nights, it just doesn't happen."

It was Carlyle's turn to laugh. "Well, darling, I hope this is one of the good nights. Are you off home, then?"

"Yeah, as soon as I finish here." She turned her attention back to her dinner. "At least I don't have a half-hour drive anymore."

"Ah, yes. You made the move out of the suburbs."

"Queens isn't a suburb."

"My apologies."

"It's crazy, though," she said. "My whole life I hear how expensive it is to live in Manhattan, and I found this really nice place, half the cost of what I'd expect."

"That's a stroke of luck."

"Close to work, too," she said. "Hell, I can walk there from here. But you already know that, don't you? Corky knows where I live, and he can't keep his mouth shut."

"He can be discreet," Carlyle said. "When he chooses."

"I've never seen him do it," she said. "But y'know, for a while I thought he'd gotten me the place. As a favor, right? But he swears he didn't. And anyway, I didn't hear about it through him. It was a cop who pointed me in the right direction. And the really crazy thing? It was—"

Carlyle gave her a moment to finish. She didn't. "Erin, darling," he said. "Perhaps there's a point to this story, but I can't say until you've come to the end."

"Bob," she said softly. "Bob Michaelson." She looked up at Carlyle. "He's the—"

"Don't say it," Carlyle said quickly. "Not here."

A few heads were pointed her way, and some of them were guys she'd pegged as mob thugs. She nodded her understanding.

But they both knew it was true. Michaelson had O'Malley connections. He'd known about the apartment and he'd known about Rüdel. That was why he'd requested the shift change to cover the warehouse, and why he'd gone there with Hendricks. None of it was a coincidence. Michaelson was the mob mole in Precinct 8. He was the guy Lieutenant Keane was looking for.

"Shit," Erin said. "I have to go." She got up, leaving her stew half-finished. Rolf jumped up beside her, ready to follow.

Carlyle put a hand on her arm. "Erin, this isn't as important as finding our German lad."

"Yeah? I can't find him," she said, shaking him off. "But I can do this. Think about what I asked you, okay?"

"I'll get word to you," Carlyle promised. "But be careful, lass."

"Everyone keeps telling me that."

"Aye, but I mean it more than the rest of them."

* * *

One of the things Erin liked about Rolf was that he didn't need explanations. He didn't worry that they were going back to the precinct instead of home. He was just glad to be included. He was ready to work until he dropped, just like her.

The precinct was humming with activity. The Civic Center wasn't in the Eightball's area of responsibility, but that didn't mean there was nothing going on. Every urban police station was busy overnight. Crime didn't stop when the sun went down; quite the opposite. Erin dodged past the usual procession of Patrol officers and handcuffed perps, making her way upstairs.

Major Crimes wasn't empty either.

"What are you doing here?" Erin asked, surprised.

Kira looked up from her desk. "Oh, you came back, too?"

"I'm following up on something." Erin sat down at her desk and logged onto her computer.

"Rüdel?"

"No."

Kira sighed. "Erin, you still pissed at me? About the O'Malley thing?"

Honesty came easier than diplomacy to Erin. "Yeah, I guess I am. You bailed on me."

"We've got a terrorist to catch!" Kira exclaimed. "We don't have time for a mole hunt."

Erin glanced around the office. They were the only two on the floor. From downstairs came the sound of some sort of scuffle. Probably a couple of drunken assholes. "I know who it is," she said in a lower tone.

"What?"

"You heard me."

"Okay. Who?"

Erin shook her head. "What, now you want to know? What happened to letting me crash and burn?"

"Wow. You are still pissed."

"I told you I was!"

"You're kind of a bitch sometimes, you know that?"

"Why are you even here?"

"I told you! There's a terrorist to catch!"

"No, I mean, why the hell are you in Major Crimes?"

Kira scowled. "The hell are you talking about?"

"You don't like fieldwork. You're scared out of your wits when there's guns involved. You do your best work behind a desk. Why don't you go back to Internal Affairs? Seems like you'd be happy there."

"Maybe I will! If you help me catch a dirty cop, like you say you're doing!"

They stared at each other. Rolf was on his feet, watching his partner warily. He could tell she was upset.

"Okay," Erin said, putting up one of her hands. "You want in, come on, damn it all. But you're not gonna like it."

"That ought to make you happy," Kira said, standing up and coming over to Erin's desk. "You'll be making me miserable. Who are we looking at?"

"Bob Michaelson."

"Bullshit."

"I'm serious. He's been getting info from the O'Malleys."

"So have you."

"Right," Erin admitted. "But I know I'm not the mole."

"Oh yeah, that'll stand up in court."

Erin rolled her eyes. "Just listen, okay? He switched shifts the day of the shooting. I think he got a tipoff about Rüdel and was trying to get him."

"That all you got?"

"He also got me my apartment."

"What?"

"When I moved to Manhattan. He aimed me at a place with the rent half what it should've been. That should've been a red flag. I think the O'Malleys meant it as a thank-you for saving the Barley Corner from that bomb last summer."

Kira was staring at her again. "You took a payoff from the mob?"

"No! I didn't know they were involved until about fifteen minutes ago!"

"They expect you to do something in return?"

"If they did, they'd probably have told me they'd done me the favor in the first place," Erin said dryly.

"Okay," Kira said. "So what? Taking a tip from an informant about a wanted felon isn't illegal, Erin. Neither is helping another officer find a place to live."

"I know. That's why we need to pull Michaelson's cases."

"All of them? Jesus, Erin, the guy's been a cop half his life!"

Erin nodded. "We need a smoking gun, that's all. Just enough to get IAB looking in the right place. They'll build the case."

"So you want to look at his major stuff?"

"Yeah. Anything connected to the O'Malleys, especially."

"Time for an archive dive, then," Kira said. "I'll see what I can find."

"You okay with putting the Rüdel thing on hold for tonight?"

"What choice do we have?" Kira replied. "I'm just here 'cause I can't sleep."

"Digging through old case files ought to take care of that," Erin said, managing a thin smile. "Sure cure for insomnia."

Chapter 18

Erin was right about wanting to sleep. Three hours of scanning old case files left her eyelids drooping. The NYPD had started to digitize its archives, but a lot of the closed cases were still filed the old-fashioned way. That meant looking through physical folders, stapled and clipped together, with all the case documentation on one side and pink and blue carbon DD-5 forms on the other. The DD-5 was a form detectives used to flesh out the original 61 complaint form, which was another piece of paper Erin knew all too well from her time on Patrol.

Her dad had told her once that the better you got at police work, the worse the work itself got. She'd thought he was talking about the cases themselves; once a cop made detective, the really heinous shit got dumped on them. But he could've just as accurately meant the paperwork. Detectives practically swam in the stuff.

Kira and Erin took turns going down to the file room for more boxes of case files, most of which were useless. Bob Michaelson was just one officer in a precinct which had employed hundreds of police over the years. He wasn't a detective, which made it harder to separate the complaints he'd handled from the rest of the pile. And, of course, most of what he'd done was small stuff. The main calls a Patrol officer answered were noise complaints, disorderly conducts, and domestic disputes, none of which had anything to do with organized crime.

"We're doing this wrong," Kira announced.

"You're saying this *now*?" Erin snapped.

"It's gonna take all night," Kira said. "Maybe all week."

"You got a better idea?"

"Maybe." Kira tapped keys on her computer. "I'm calling up Michaelson's personnel file."

"You won't have access to much of it," Erin objected. "Only IAB and his CO will have the good stuff."

"I know," Kira said. "But there still might be something." Her voice trailed off.

Erin shook her head and turned back to her current file box. She still hadn't found anything worth mentioning.

"Whoa," Kira said.

"What?" Erin was at the other woman's desk as quickly as her tired feet could get her there.

"Did you know he's a hero?"

"What are you talking about?"

"I shit you not." Kira pointed to the screen. "Look. September of '05. Fatal shooting, two officers involved. Bob Michaelson and Carl Dempsey. Two perps, both DOA."

"That's worth checking," Erin said, starting for the stairs. "I'll get the file."

The case file from the incident was thicker than most, which made sense. Officer-involved shootings got a lot of attention and required a lot more forms. According to the original complaint, Officer Michaelson and Officer Dempsey were detailed to SNEU, the Street Narcotics Enforcement Unit, at the time.

"They did a buy-and-bust on a couple Colombians connected with a South American cartel," Erin said, scanning the document. "When they moved in to make the arrest, the perps decided to fight it out. According to the officers' testimony, one of the dealers, Eduardo Garcia, drew a gun. Michaelson shot him three times, killing him instantly. The other dealer, Manuel Fernandez, was also armed. He went for a revolver in his waistband. Michaelson shot him twice. He died waiting for the paramedics."

"Killed two guys," Kira said. "Wow."

"Yeah," Erin said. She went back and read the report again. "That's strange."

"Not really," Kira said. "It was dumb to throw down on our guys when they already had guns out, but crooks are stupid."

"Not that. Dempsey."

"What about him?"

"He didn't fire his weapon."

Kira shrugged. "It happened fast. Maybe it was all over before he could get a shot off."

"No way," Erin said. "One guy, maybe. But Michaelson puts three rounds in one dealer, then shifts targets and double-taps the other one, and Dempsey just stands there?"

"Y'know, you might be right," Kira said. "You know the stats on this?"

"No, but I'm guessing you do."

Kira nodded. "Everyone who ever worked IAB knows this stat. If there's more than one officer in a shooting, every officer fires twice as many shots, on average. It's a feedback loop. But maybe Dempsey freaked out."

"Maybe he froze, sure. But I want to talk to him."

"Erin, this happened eight years ago. You think he'll be any use?"

"If you'd shot a guy eight years ago, I bet you'd remember it like it was yesterday."

Kira smiled shakily. "I've been in a gunfight."

"I don't suppose Dempsey's still at the Eightball," Erin said. "I don't recognize the name."

"Let's find out." Kira pulled up the roster. "Nope. No Dempsey here. I'll see where he transferred." She typed out a search. "Huh. He's out of the NYPD."

"Retired?"

"Permanent disability."

"We have an address? Phone number?"

"Got them both here. Looks like he's down in Brooklyn."

Erin grabbed her notepad and scribbled the address and phone number. "Okay, I'll talk to him." She straightened up. "Rolf? *Komm.*"

The Shepherd had been napping beside her desk. He scrambled to his feet and trotted to her side.

"Erin?"

"What?"

"You do know it's after midnight, right?"

"Yeah?"

"So maybe this isn't the best time to go knocking on an ex-cop's door."

"Maybe not," Erin agreed. "You think this ties in to the O'Malleys?"

"How the hell am I supposed to know that? You wanted to find something unusual in Michaelson's record. This is the biggest thing he's been involved in."

"Okay, I'll talk to Dempsey in the morning."

"You gonna have time? We're still on the Rüdel thing."

"Shit." Erin tried to think. "You know what? The hell with it." She pulled out her phone and entered the number off her pad.

"You wake him up, he's gonna be pissed," Kira warned.

Erin held up a hand. The phone was ringing.

After four rings, she was getting ready for a voicemail, but the man on the other end of the line sounded awake.

"Yeah?"

"Hello. Carl Dempsey?"

"Yeah? Who's this?"

"Sir, my name's Erin O'Reilly. I'm a detective with the NYPD. Sorry for calling so late. But there's something I need your help with."

Dempsey laughed harshly. "Lady, you're a little behind the times. Got a news flash for you. I'm off the force."

"I know," Erin said. "I need to talk to you about something that happened a while back. Could I drop by? I'm in Manhattan, but I can be at your place in twenty or thirty minutes."

There was a long pause. Then Dempsey said, "What's this about? You IAB?"

"I'm with Major Crimes," Erin said truthfully.

"Okay, why not," he said. "Bring a bottle. We'll have a little party."

"I'll be there as soon as I can," she said, ignoring his last words. "Thanks."

"Don't thank me yet, sweet cheeks," he said and hung up.

"Sweet cheeks?" she repeated into the dead phone.

"Sounds like you've got a date," Kira said.

"Shut up."

"I won't wait up for you."

"I said, shut up."

"I guess we're done for tonight." Kira stretched and yawned. "I'm dead on my feet here. If I'm gonna be good for anything tomorrow, I better catch a couple hours. You might try it yourself, if you're not too busy with your new boyfriend."

Erin didn't bother to answer. She clipped Rolf's leash onto his collar. Then the two of them rolled out of the precinct, making for Brooklyn.

* * *

Carl Dempsey lived in an old brick apartment in Gowanus. Erin took one look at the rickety elevator in the lobby and opted for the stairs. The stairwell smelled like cigarettes and stale beer. Just visiting was depressing. She couldn't imagine living there.

She rang the doorbell, waited a half-minute, and rang it again. As she was wondering if she had the right place, three bolts clicked back.

"Who's that?" the man on the other side asked.

"Detective O'Reilly," she said. "Mr. Dempsey?"

"Yeah. C'mon in." The door opened about two inches, no farther.

Erin pushed cautiously on it. Something felt a little strange about the situation. She didn't think it was an ambush, but her instincts told her to be careful. She laid a hand near the butt of her Glock and glanced down at Rolf, making sure he was alert. Then she walked in.

She felt immediately foolish. There was definitely something wrong, but it wasn't anything to be scared of. Carl Dempsey sat in front of her in a wheelchair.

They looked at one another, each aware that the other was giving a Patrol once-over. Dempsey was younger than she'd expected, about her own age. He wasn't bad-looking, but clearly hadn't been taking care of himself. Nobody looked their best at one in the morning, but Dempsey looked worse than most. He had dark bags under bloodshot eyes and a week of stubble on his chin.

"You're prettier than I expected," he said, breaking the silence.

"You're not," she shot back.

That earned her a surprised smile and a nod. He extended a hand. "Carl," he said. "I'd get up, but..."

"Erin," she said, shaking the offered hand. He had a firm grip, in spite of his appearance.

"You bring that bottle?"

She shook her head. "Sorry. I came straight from work, and you know how they are."

"That's okay," he said. "I've got my own. Pour you a cocktail?"

"Can't. I'm on the clock."

"I remember how that works," he said. "God bless disability retirement." He wheeled himself into the kitchen, where the necessary implements were already laid out. He poured a generous serving of rye whiskey into a jigger, combining it with vermouth and bitters. He stirred it and poured the drink. "You sure you don't want one?"

"No, thanks," she said. "I don't suppose you've got any instant coffee?"

"Long night, hey? Sorry, don't drink much coffee these days. But there's Coke in the fridge if you want. Help yourself."

Caffeine might keep her sharp. She took a can out of the refrigerator and popped the tab. Dempsey slugged back half his Manhattan at one go.

"We'll talk in the living room," he said.

It was obvious he lived alone. Everything about the apartment said "bachelor pad." Clothes were strewn on the furniture, a couple empty bottles on the coffee table. Those bottles reminded Erin of Michaelson's apartment and the reason she'd come.

"Carl, I'd like to hear about something that happened back when you were on the Job," she said, taking a seat on a seedy old couch.

He pivoted the wheelchair into a corner so he was facing her. "Nice K-9 you got there. I feel like I'm the one who should have a dog. You wanna lend him to me? He could be my assistance animal."

"He's not trained for that," she said. "And he mostly speaks German."

"That so? Well, I guess he's not called an American Shepherd." Carl laughed a little too loudly at his own joke and took another swallow of his cocktail.

"It's about the dual shooting you were involved in, back in '05," she said, trying to steer the conversation back on track.

"I never shot anybody," he said. "Never even fired my weapon at a perp. Not once."

"I know. That's what I wanted to ask you about."

"Huh?"

"Why didn't you shoot Fernandez and Garcia?"

"What, they weren't dead enough already? You think I should've popped 'em a couple times, just to show I was a team player?"

"So Michaelson was faster than you on the draw?"

"What's it matter? They were assholes, right? Now they're dead assholes, and they've been dead almost a decade, so fuck 'em."

Erin narrowed her eyes. "What do you mean?"

"You read the report, so why are you asking me? It's all in there."

"And that's how it went down? No different?"

"You think I lied in my statement?" Dempsey tossed back the rest of his drink and slapped the empty glass down on the table. "The hell with you. You said you weren't Internal Affairs."

"I'm not," she said. "But Bob Michaelson's in trouble, and you were his partner. I need to find out how far back the trouble goes, so I can help him."

"Bob's in trouble?" Carl laughed again, but it wasn't a cheerful sound. "Why the hell would I want to pull his chestnuts out of the fire?"

"You were partners," she said again.

"Oh, yeah, brothers in blue," he snorted. "The goddamn blue wall. Yeah, I know. Screw it, screw him, screw the whole goddamn NYPD. What the hell has it done for me? One-third salary for disability. You think I can live on that? In goddamn New York City?"

"How'd you end up in that chair?" she asked.

"Motorcycle accident," he said. "Drunk asshole wiped me out at a stoplight two years ago. Wasn't line of duty, they said, so tough titty. One-third pay."

"You got family?"

He snorted again. "Wife packed up last year. She said it was because I was drinking. I think it was the chair, she wanted a guy with all the moving parts. Whatever. Maybe I had it coming."

She leaned forward. "Carl, why did you have it coming? You didn't shoot anyone, like you told me."

"I sure as shit didn't stop them getting shot, either."

Erin's heart was pounding. "You've got a story to tell here. You want to tell it to someone."

"You want a bedtime story?" he asked with a sarcastic smile. "Okay, here it is. Once upon a time, there was a little boy who wanted to be a cop. He saw all the movies, and the TV shows, and thought how great it'd be to help people. The little boy was this dipshit idealist who believed all the bullshit. You know the motto: *fidelis ad mortem*."

"Faithful unto death," Erin translated. Every NYPD officer knew it.

"Right. They don't say what happens if you're unlucky enough not to die. Anyway, the little boy grew up, or at least he got bigger. All the other little boys who'd wanted to be firefighters and astronauts and policemen ended up dentists and lawyers and CPAs, but he still wanted to be a cop. So he took all the classes, went to the Academy, graduated number fifteen in his class. And y'know what? When they played "New York, New York" at graduation, he cried. He actually cried, he was so happy.

"They'd told him the Job wasn't like it was on TV, of course. And it wasn't. It was better. Because it was real people, and every now and then, the boy was able to help them. He got to know the folks on his beat, learned about their problems, talked to them, got good at the Job. He had a partner who was good police, a guy who'd been doing it a few years, who knew what was what. They got on okay.

"Then they went in on a B&B for a drug crew. These mopes were some bad operators, cartel guys. The little boy and his partner busted them, pure textbook. It was righteous, they had 'em cold."

Dempsey stopped talking. He just sat and stared at the tabletop, remembering. Erin let him take his time. She'd been in enough interrogations to know when not to push.

"That's when the little boy grew up," he finally said. "That's when he learned what was bullshit. And you know what? Everything is."

Erin nodded and waited.

"The mopes had guns," Dempsey said quietly. "That was true. But they didn't go for them. The boy's partner didn't give them the chance."

Erin swallowed. She was hearing something she really didn't want to be true. But she'd gone looking for it, and she had to see it through now. "He executed them," she said around the lump in her throat.

He nodded. "They had their hands in the air," he whispered, and the look in his eyes when he raised his head was something Erin knew she'd remember as long as she lived.

"You didn't know it was going to happen," she said.

"I should've known," he said miserably. "There were signs, y'know? He was taking calls from this guy, stuff about the drug business. He said it was a CI, right? But he didn't handle him like a CI. It was a different power dynamic, like the other guy was in charge. He'd never tell me anything about him."

"This guy," Erin said. "He have a name?"

"He called him Tommy."

"Tommy Jay O'Malley?" she suggested.

He shrugged. "Could be. I never met the guy."

"You think Bob shot those two to take out another dealer's rivals?"

Dempsey nodded. He had tears in his eyes. "Yeah. I do."

"And you know for sure the perps weren't going for their weapons?"

He nodded again.

"Will you say that? If someone from IAB does ask, later?"

"What's the point?"

"The point?" she echoed. Now she was pissed off. "The point is, you saw two guys get murdered. I thought you said you believed in the police!"

"I did!" he retorted. "But what the hell does it matter? That investigation was closed. Eight years ago. If I speak up now, it's one cop's word against the other. There's no goddamn evidence. He walks, and I look like an asshole. I could lose my disability. And that's assuming no one comes after me!"

"This is eating you up," she said, shifting on the couch so she was a little closer to his wheelchair. "You're blaming yourself for this. It wasn't your fault, Carl."

"Like hell," he said. "I could've done something, said something."

"You just did. My dad once said, 'It's never too late to do the right thing.'"

"Your dad? Was he on the Job, too?"

"Twenty-five years."

"He good police?"

"The best."

Dempsey nodded. "Christ, I didn't want any of this," he said, making a gesture with one hand that took in his apartment, his wheelchair, his career, and his life all at once.

"I have evidence that Michaelson's been working for the O'Malley mob on the side," she said. "His current partner got killed because of it. You know about that?"

He closed his eyes. "Yeah, I heard."

"Help me make this right, Carl." She put out a hand and touched the back of his wrist. "Remember that little boy who wanted to wear the shield. What would he want you to do?"

Dempsey's eyes were still closed. When he spoke, it was so quiet she had to lean close to hear him.

"Okay. I'll do it. I'll make your damn statement."

Chapter 19

Erin didn't even want to think about what time it was when she left Dempsey's apartment. The sun would be coming up soon, and she had a long day in front of her. She wondered if it was even worth trying to get any sleep. The drive from Brooklyn to Manhattan convinced her it was, when she almost nodded off in the middle of the Battery Tunnel. Another driver's irritated honk snapped her awake when she drifted over a line.

"Stupid," she muttered. What had she been thinking, chasing the Michaelson case? There was no rush on it, and she'd wasted hours of time and energy she might need. It had been simple frustration. Erin would rather be doing than waiting.

By the time she got to her apartment, the sky was turning pink. Taking Dempsey's statement, together with her drive, had eaten up the night. Erin set her alarm two hours in the future, stripped off her clothes, and tumbled into bed.

The alarm went off about thirty seconds later, by the feel of it. She tumbled out of bed and into the shower, threw on a fresh blouse and slacks, grabbed a protein bar, and hustled Rolf out the door. There wasn't time for her morning run. The Commissioner's press conference was set for noon, Hendricks's funeral two hours later. That gave her the morning to sort things out.

"Glad you could join us, O'Reilly," Webb said as she hurried into Major Crimes. "Hope you slept well."

She stared at him blankly, wondering if he was joking. Then she remembered he didn't know what she'd been doing the night before. "We get anything on Rüdel?" she asked, angling in on the break room and its blessed coffee machine.

"Nothing," Vic growled.

"Where's Homeland Security?" Erin asked. Just the smell of the coffee was enough to perk her up a little.

"One PP," Webb said.

"With about half the NYPD," Vic added. "The other half's pounding pavement looking for this asshole. So what've you been up to?"

Kira gave Erin a sidelong look but didn't say anything.

Erin decided, the hell with it. She took out a folded packet of paper and handed it to Webb.

"What's this?" he asked.

"Witness statement."

Webb unfolded it and looked at the top page. "Carl Dempsey? Who's he?"

"Former cop."

Webb nodded and skimmed the page. "Dead drug dealers? I don't see what—"

Erin gave him a moment to finish his sentence. He didn't. He just kept staring at the paper.

"I saw a guy have that happen to him once," Vic said, pointing a thumb at the Lieutenant. "Construction accident. A piece of rebar fell twelve stories, went straight through the sidewalk two feet in front of him. Took him three and a half minutes—"

"Vic," Kira said gently, "no one cares."

"Holy shit," Webb said in a near-whisper. "You know what you've got here, O'Reilly?"

"Murder and conspiracy," she said.

"Implicating the partner of the guy whose funeral we'll be attending a few hours from now," he said. "That's some fantastic sense of timing you got there. You were working this as a side case?"

"Yeah." No point denying it.

"When were you planning on telling me?"

"When I had something solid."

Webb chewed his lower lip thoughtfully. "Well, this is solid, all right." He turned to the rest of the squad. "Either of you know anything about this?"

Vic shook his head.

Kira reluctantly nodded. "I've been helping."

"Jesus. Don't you people have enough to do stopping the terrorists?"

"What are we supposed to do about that?" Erin retorted.

"We could be four pairs of boots at the Civic Center, or walking the subway tunnels," Vic suggested.

"We've got guys all over the place down there," Webb sighed. "K-9s, too. I think every dog the city's got is either underground or working checkpoints, except yours."

"Rüdel doesn't have any associates we can lean on," Kira said.

"Except Thomas O'Malley," Erin said.

"The Irish are trying to kill Rüdel," Vic said. "Talking to them isn't gonna help us."

"I'm going to take another look at his file," Kira said. "Maybe it'll give me some ideas."

"The rest of you, start calling informants," Webb said. "See if there's anyone, anyone at all, who has any idea where this son of a bitch is. Start at the top of the list and work your way down."

"What about Michaelson?" Erin asked.

"What about him?" Webb shot back. "He's not going anywhere. That shooting was years ago. We've got more immediate problems. We'll bring him in once this is all over."

It was a waste of time, but they didn't have any better ideas. They started calling every lowlife, small-time crook, and addict who might know anything and who owed the NYPD a favor. Half the numbers had been disconnected, and ninety percent of the rest were useless or hostile. All they got was vague rumors and the sort of sighting report people gave when they thought they were telling a cop what the detective wanted to hear.

And all the time, the hands on the wall clock kept going round. Erin looked at it every few minutes, wondering what Carlyle was up to and whether he'd come up with anything. She resisted the urge to call him. If he had something for her, he'd let her know.

Carlyle. There was a thought.

"Maybe there's another way we can do this," she said. "We're not the only ones looking for Rüdel."

"You mean the Irish?" Kira asked.

Erin didn't answer. Instead, she turned to Webb. "We've been monitoring security cams in the subways, right?"

"Twenty-four seven," he confirmed. "Hell, there's a guy from Homeland watching feeds right now."

"The cameras are in color, right?"

"The hell difference does it make?" Vic asked. "What are you looking for?"

Erin smiled slightly. "A redhead."

Webb got it. "Finneran?"

"Yeah," Erin said. "She's hunting him, damn near got him once that we know of. She may still have a line on him."

Vic laughed. "You're a born K-9 officer, Erin. Treating another perp like your tracker dog."

Webb didn't laugh. "Worth a try," he said. "But the Homeland guys aren't gonna like going back through all that footage. They won't remember any of it."

"Sir, don't think like a cop, think like a man," Erin said.

"Huh?"

"You know how much of our time women spend walking around, knowing sleazy jerks are checking us out? You saw Siobhan. What'd you think of her?"

Webb shrugged.

"Come on, sir," she said, exasperated.

"She's gorgeous," he said.

"Yeah," Erin agreed. "Any straight guy saw her, he's gonna remember."

"What if the surveillance cops are women?" Vic asked.

"Women notice other women," Kira said. "Go into a gas station, check out the girly mags."

"Every time," Vic said, grinning.

"Then look at the women's health mags," Kira went on. "Look at the covers. What do you see?"

"Hot women," Vic said.

"Crazy world, isn't it," Kira said.

Webb took out his phone and called Agent Smith. He explained their theory. Then they had to wait a half hour while Smith called his underlings.

"This doesn't bother you?" Vic asked Erin while they waited.

"What?"

"Using base impulses to catch bad guys?" Kira asked. "Don't we do that all the time?"

"Yeah," he said. "But you're using *cops'* base impulses."

"We have to put up with it," Erin said. "Might as well use it to do some good."

"You're a cold, hard bitch," he said. "And I love you for it."

Webb's phone buzzed. "Webb," he answered. "Yeah? Really? Where? Okay, thanks."

They stared at him.

"I asked Smith to check with all his electronic surveillance guys," Webb said. "He's got people on traffic cams, security footage, you name it. I asked him about a pretty redhead showing up on the cameras. You were right, O'Reilly. One of his boys remembers a girl matching that description."

"Where?" Erin asked.

"Nowhere helpful. Rental-car place at La Guardia."

"So she rented a car," Vic said. "What's that got to do with anything?"

"We'll know in a minute," Webb said. "Smith's uploading the camera footage now."

Soon they were clustered around Webb's desk, staring at his computer screen.

"Why's Homeland watching car-rental joints?" Kira asked.

"They're covering the airports," Webb said. "The rentals are a long shot, but we don't want to miss any chance."

The camera resolution wasn't great. Webb squinted at the screen and fast-forwarded. It took a few minutes, but the flash of long, red hair was unmistakable. He rewound and played it again, normal speed.

"That's her," Erin said.

"No audio, of course," Vic muttered.

Siobhan approached the counter. Even through the grainy image, they could see the clerk behind it was very taken with her. She leaned forward, twisting a strand of hair around one of her fingers.

"She's flirting," Kira said.

"Probably pumping him for information," Erin said.

"Jones, get down to La Guardia," Webb said. He glanced at the clock. "We've got an hour and a half to the press conference. I need answers. Find that rental-car clerk and learn what Finneran asked about, and what he told her. Every damn word. You got that?"

Kira nodded.

"Go," Webb said. She was out the door in seconds.

"I don't get it," Vic said. "What's she need a rental car for?"

"She doesn't," Erin said. "She's looking for Rüdel."

"And he's rented a car?" Vic snorted. "That's not his style. Remember last time? All his cars were stolen."

Erin was still watching the security feed

Siobhan was sitting on the edge of the counter now, giving the clerk a coy look over her shoulder. He said something and she threw back her head in apparent laughter. Then she neatly pivoted and slid down on his side of the counter. He seemed to be protesting, but she put a fingertip against his lips and that shut him up. She leaned around him and looked at his computer screen.

Siobhan gave the hapless clerk a quick kiss on the cheek and swung herself back over the counter again. Then she was gone, leaving the clerk standing there looking like he'd taken a two-by-four between the eyes.

"She got what she came for," Erin reported.

"But what is it?" Webb demanded.

"It's gotta be Rüdel's transport," Vic said.

"He's been getting around in the sewers and subway tunnels," Webb reminded him. "On foot, or in a boat."

"Yeah, but we know that now," Erin said. "And he knows we know. He wants to get away after this is over."

"The car's for his exit," Webb said. "He probably had one of his guys set up the rental. How'd Finneran know about it?"

"Does it matter?" Vic asked. "We can ask her if we catch her. But she's not exactly our priority right now."

"Okay," Webb said, standing up. "Neshenko, O'Reilly, I want both of you at One PP. Jones may be able to get us the make, model, and plates of whatever car Finneran was interested in."

"Where are you gonna be?" Vic asked.

"I'd better come with you. Smooth things over with Homeland."

"Sir?" Erin asked.

"Yes?"

"Finding the getaway vehicle won't help us stop an attack."

The look Webb gave her was tired but unyielding. "I know. But it's all we've got. Now let's move."

Chapter 20

"Well, this is gonna look great on the evening news," Vic muttered.

"You're not kidding," Erin said.

Number One Police Plaza looked like a fortress. ESU officers in full tactical gear were deployed all around the building, a pair of Bearcat armored cars idling at curbside. Uniformed officers were everywhere, interspersed with Federal agents. Sharpshooters' heads and rifle barrels poked over the edges of neighboring roofs. Cameramen, waiting to get into the press room, were snapping pictures of the police.

Webb was on the phone with Agent Smith. He signed off and hung up. "Okay, O'Reilly," he said to Erin. "Your K-9's a bomb-sniffer, so you'll have him on perimeter duty. They want you on the west side, checking foot traffic. Neshenko, you're with her. I'll be at the front door. Keep in contact."

"Yes, sir," Erin said. She, Vic, and Rolf walked briskly to the brick and stone plaza just west of the headquarters building and joined the officers there. They showed their IDs to the Patrol Lieutenant in charge and started moving along the edge of the crowd of spectators. New Yorkers liked a show, and a big crowd of bystanders had gathered.

"I feel like I'm in friggin' Baghdad," Vic said. The detectives had put on their body armor, including Rolf's K-9 vest, and Vic was carrying his M4 rifle. "You think this asshole's really gonna show? I mean, if he does, no way does he walk away from this."

Erin shrugged. She was watching her dog. "*Such,*" she told Rolf. He obediently put his nose to the bricks. Tail wagging, he sniffed his way across the plaza, looking for bombs.

Vic scanned the crowd. He held his rifle at his shoulder, the muzzle pointing diagonally down across his body. "Shit," he said. "There's gotta be a thousand people here. Goddamn rubberneckers."

"Vic," Erin said. "Do you ever stop bitching?"

He cracked a smile. "Only once the shooting starts."

* * *

They worked the plaza until just before noon with no result. Webb didn't pass along any word from Kira. A Patrol officer brought them coffee, but they kept moving while they drank it, guarding the perimeter. Then, walking just outside the row of potted bushes on the plaza, Rolf suddenly stopped and sat, bolt upright, staring at a guy with a backpack.

"Vic!" Erin hissed. The guy didn't look like much, just a kid really. He was maybe sixteen years old. But Rolf was giving a firm positive.

"Hey, you!" Vic snapped. His rifle came up.

The kid's eyes widened. He started to turn away.

"Get down on the ground! Now!" Vic shouted.

"Everybody down!" Erin called to the crowd. If there was a bomb, and it went off now, it'd probably wipe out a couple dozen bystanders. Her Glock was in her hand without even thinking about it. She trained it on the kid.

Some of the civilians, maybe half, listened to her and got down. The rest stood and stared like a bunch of idiots.

The boy dropped to the ground on his stomach. Vic and Erin closed with him, guns ready.

"Spread your hands!" Vic ordered. "Let me see 'em!"

The kid was trying to say something, but he was terrified. He couldn't get any words out.

"Shut up!" Vic said. "Stay down! Don't move!"

Erin stood over him. "What's in the pack?" she demanded.

"No... nothing," he stammered.

"Bullshit! What's in there?"

"Just... just a... a prank," he managed to say.

More cops were moving over. Vic waved them back. If the kid was lying, he didn't want more people up close. They'd just increase the casualty count.

Erin dropped to one knee beside the kid, keeping out of his field of view in case he tried anything. She looked at the backpack. It didn't look dangerous, but she'd handled a bomb once before and it wasn't an experience she wanted to repeat. "What sort of prank?"

"It's... a couple M-80s," he said weakly.

"Jesus Christ," Vic said in exasperation. "You've got *firecrackers* in there?"

The kid's head moved about half an inch in a hint of a nod.

"How goddamn stupid can you be?" Vic demanded. "Did you want to get shot?"

Erin looked at the kid. She was pretty sure he was telling the truth. She could hold him and wait for the bomb squad, but that might pull the explosives guys away from somewhere else they really needed to be. She inched the pack's zipper open just wide enough for one finger and probed inside. Finding no wires or any hint of an anti-tampering device, she eased the pack open. "Keep still," she told the kid.

What she found was exactly what the boy had said. Two small, red cylinders with fuses sticking out of them. As she pulled them out, she saw a bright flash in the corner of her eye. She turned and saw a photographer in the act of taking their picture.

"Great," she sighed. She and Vic could look forward to a photo of them holding a scared kid at gunpoint, all over a stupid prank. "We're clear," she said to Vic.

The kid shifted, getting ready to get up.

"Stay down," she snapped at him. "What's your name?"

"Nathan."

"Nathan what?"

"Renwick."

"Okay, Nathan Renwick," she said. "You're under arrest for illegal possession of fireworks. You have the right to remain silent..."

By the time she'd finished reading Nathan his rights, three uniformed officers had approached to take him into custody. The handcuffed kid was led away. He'd recovered enough to start protesting.

"Fantastic," Vic said. "Two hundred cops here, and you just got a sorry-ass misdemeanor collar. Great use of police resources. Congrats, Detective. They'll probably give you a medal."

"If they do, I know where you can stick it," Erin said. The rush of adrenaline was subsiding and she was remembering just how little sleep she'd had. "What time is it?"

"Ten to noon," Vic said. "Conference'll be starting soon."

"Hey, Officers?"

They turned. A bicycle courier had approached.

"Yeah?" Erin asked.

"I have a delivery for a Detective O'Reilly," he said. He pointed a thumb back toward the headquarters building. "They wouldn't let me in, but this guy in a trench coat told me O'Reilly was over here."

"What's the delivery?" she asked.

"Ma'am, I don't look in the envelopes. Are you Detective O'Reilly? Or is he?"

"That's me." She flashed her ID. "Who's it from?"

The courier gave her an odd look. "Delivery slip says, 'An old friend.' If you could sign here?"

She scribbled her signature on the delivery slip. He handed her a padded envelope with something small and solid inside. "Have a nice day, ma'am." He mounted his bike and pedaled off.

"You really wanna mess with that?" Vic asked, raising an eyebrow.

"If it was a bomb, Rolf would tell me," she said, tearing the envelope open. The only things inside were a cheap flip-phone and a folded slip of paper. The paper had a phone number printed on it. Ignoring Vic, she opened the phone and dialed the number.

"Good morning, darling," Carlyle said.

"What's going on?" she demanded.

"We've no time for idle chatter," he said. "I've made inquiries, and I've a notion what our friend is up to."

"What?"

"Corky talked to some lads he knows. Apparently, in addition to the missing inventory from Connaught Imports, a significant quantity of ANFO is missing from the inventory of Emerald Isles Estates. Are you acquainted with the substance?"

"Yeah," Erin said. Her stomach felt suddenly hollow. "That's the stuff they used in '95 in Oklahoma City."

"Aye, and we used it a great deal in the Troubles," he agreed. "Now, taking everything together, this gives our lad a great deal of blasting power, but it's in rather a large package, difficult to transport."

"He can't get a truck bomb in here," she said. "There's roadblocks all over the place."

"Aye. But with that much explosive, he needn't be inside the building."

"Listen to me," she said. "He can't even get close. Oh shit, are we guarding the wrong building?"

"Nay, I think you're in the right place," Carlyle said. "But he needn't be approaching from above."

"He's been working underground the whole time," Erin agreed. "But he couldn't smuggle a bomb into One PP's basement. It doesn't connect to anything."

"How well do you know the subway system?"

"Not too well." Erin had grown up in Queens and hadn't spent a lot of time in Manhattan.

"The Lexington Avenue line runs just under City Hall."

"Vic," Erin called, waving him over. "You know the Lexington Avenue subway line?"

"Yeah. We're pretty much on top of it..." He trailed off.

"Darling? Are you listening?" Carlyle asked.

"City Hall Loop," Vic said. "The old station. It's right under our feet. Are you saying...?"

"City Hall Loop," Erin echoed into the phone.

"Aye," Carlyle said. "I've been looking at the blueprints, and it's likely a large enough device, placed properly, might bring down the building. At the least, it could collapse the plaza. I'm watching the television now, and there appear to be a great many New Yorkers there."

"And I'm one of them," Erin said. "Thanks." She snapped the phone shut without another word. As she did, she saw the clock on the screen. It read 11:58.

"Vic, we have to move *right now*."

*   *   *

They ran. As they went, Erin speed-dialed Webb with one hand.

"Was that you, with the bomb scare?" he asked by way of greeting.

"Forget about it," she said. "I got a tip, Rüdel might be in the old City Hall subway station. We're going there now."

They arrived at the subway entrance. A couple of uniforms were guarding the stairs.

"What's up, Detectives?" one of the Patrol cops asked.

"You guys, with me," Vic snapped.

"On what authority?" the other cop asked.

Vic didn't have time to argue jurisdiction. "Mine." He and Erin didn't wait to see if they'd follow. The detectives took the stairs two at a time. Rolf loped alongside, making it look easy.

"Send backup," Erin said into her phone.

"I'm on it," Webb said. The signal was breaking up. "You run... anything... hang back... for... cavalry."

"No time," she said, but her phone beeped and the connection cut out. "Dammit." She shoved it into a hip pocket. Glancing over her shoulder, she saw that at least the two patrolmen had followed.

The subway station had more cops on the platform, half a dozen or so, along with about twenty civilians. Fortunately, there wasn't a train at the moment.

"Get these people out of here!" Erin called to the Patrol sergeant.

"Who the hell are you?" he replied in classic New York style.

"O'Reilly, Major Crimes," she snapped. "We've got a credible bomb threat. Do your damn job."

"Okay, people," the uniform called to the bystanders. "We need you to move to the nearest exit. Calmly, please."

The detectives ignored the unfolding evacuation. "Which way?" Erin asked Vic.

"Down the tracks. First left."

They hopped off the platform onto the gravel beside the tracks. Erin had a momentary worry about the third rail, but Rolf was sticking close to her hip, true to his training. She drew her Glock again and did a quick chamber check to make sure a round was loaded and ready. The other two cops were still with them, but they looked a little uncertain.

"Maybe we should wait here—" one began.

Vic gave him a quick, contemptuous look. "Yeah, maybe you should."

Red-faced, the Patrol cop shut up and drew his gun.

The tunnel was lit with widely-spaced yellow lamps set high in the walls. They gave a sickly glow that didn't illuminate much. Some of the bulbs had burned out, others were flickering. One of the uniforms took out his flashlight.

"Put that away," Vic snapped as soon as he saw the beam.

Erin understood. The flashlights would just tell Rüdel they were coming and give him a target.

The left turn was completely dark. Metal rails, spotted with rust, dissolved into blackness. Erin shifted her grip on her gun. The air was cold, but her palms were sweating. She couldn't help thinking about the last time she'd been underground. Rüdel had very nearly killed her. She swallowed and kept moving forward.

"Do trains still run these tracks?" she hissed to Vic.

"Yeah," he replied quietly. "It's a turning loop for the Number Six trains. But they don't stop."

"Good. Means no tripwires on the tracks."

She only barely saw him nod.

Erin's world shrank down a radius of about a yard on all sides. The crunch of the gravel under her shoes was very loud in her ears. She kept putting one foot in front of the other. She wondered what they'd do if a train came along. She dropped one hand to her side and felt the comforting warmth of Rolf's head.

A weird, blue light came into view around the corner. Erin thought of stained-glass windows in her childhood church. She saw a glint of metal overhead and recognized it as a brass chandelier. This was the fanciest subway station she'd ever seen, in the heart of the biggest city in North America, and it was dark and deserted. It was one of the eeriest places she'd ever been.

"There oughta be lights," Vic muttered.

They were at the platform now. Erin could see the blue light really was stained glass in the ceiling, letting in a little filtered daylight. She cautiously climbed up onto the concrete. Vic stayed beside the tracks. The two patrolmen joined Erin on the platform.

"I don't see anybody," one of the uniforms said doubtfully.

"Rolf," Erin said. "*Such.*"

Rolf obediently put his nose to the ground, started forward, and almost immediately sat in his alert posture, staring.

Erin froze. There, lined up neatly, were three rows of metal drums, the big fifty-five gallon ones. Thin black wires ran out of them, bundled together with zip-ties.

"Holy shit," she whispered. She'd found the explosives Carlyle had been talking about.

"Dispatch, we've got a 10-33 at the City Hall Loop," one of the Patrol cops said into his radio. "We need the Bomb Squad to—"

"Get down!" Vic shouted, an instant before Erin saw the men. There were two of them, dressed in black, in the stairwell halfway down the platform. They'd been coming down the stairs when Vic spotted them.

Erin reflexively dropped to her stomach, even before she'd registered the object in the first guy's hands. A split second later, muzzle flashes lit up the subway like a golden strobe light. The man was holding some kind of submachine-gun. It fired so fast she couldn't distinguish the individual gunshots. The sound was like tearing canvas.

The patrolman on Erin's right pitched over backward, his words cut off mid-sentence. She distinctly heard the crack of his head against the floor. The other uniform dove toward the wall. Bullets chewed into the concrete and brickwork.

Erin brought her Glock in line. As she did, the flat, hard crack of Vic's rifle cut through the rattle of the automatic weapon. He fired three quick shots, then two more. Erin braced her arms on the station floor and squeezed off a shot in the direction of the gunfire.

The submachine-gun stopped firing, whether because it was out of ammo or because the shooter was down, but more muzzle flashes flared in the stairwell. These were coming from a pistol, single shots. One hit the ground just in front of Erin, stinging her face with chips of concrete. She fired four times where she'd seen the shots. Spent cartridges, still smoking, skittered over the edge of the platform.

The remaining Patrol officer was shouting into his radio, repeating "10-13! 10-13! Shots fired!" over and over. Erin wished he'd shut up.

Vic was firing steadily and methodically, like a man hammering nails. He was moving slowly forward, opening the angle with the stairwell, driving the other gunman back into cover. The shooter fired several more shots which spattered harmlessly across the platform. Erin guessed he was shooting blind. She didn't have a clear shot.

She gathered her legs under herself. "Rolf!" she shouted. "*Fass!*"

Hearing the "bite" command, the K-9 snarled and rushed the stairwell. It would've been suicidal for a human to charge an armed man like that, across twenty yards of open ground, but Rolf was smaller, lower, and much, much faster than any human sprinter. It took him something less than two seconds to cross the platform.

The gunman got off one more shot and missed. Then Rolf was in the air, flinging himself into the guy. Man and dog went down in a tangle.

Erin was up now, running forward. Vic was right behind her. She couldn't see the other cop. She had a momentary glimpse of Rolf wrestling with the perp. The idiot was actually trying to fight the dog. He had Rolf in a headlock with one arm. The other was in the Shepherd's mouth. Rolf was raking his hind legs against the man's chest and stomach, growling. His tail was wagging, but it was excitement, not friendliness.

Then something slammed into Erin's shoulder and spun her halfway around. She heard a crack, then two more.

Disoriented, she found herself leaning against the wall of the station. Vic was in front of her, rifle up, firing. He turned to look at her.

"You okay? You good?"

"Yeah," she said. Dimly, she realized she'd been shot. There ought to be pain, but there wasn't any.

"He's in the restroom!" Vic shouted.

That didn't make any sense. "What?"

"Rüdel! He's in the goddamn restroom!"

Then she got it. Rüdel had been in the bathroom and had taken a shot at her from the doorway. It was a little further down from the stairwell. She hadn't even noticed that door in the shadows.

"Good!" she called back. "There's only one way out. We've got him cornered!"

"What if he's got a detonator in there?"

"Did you hit him?"

"I don't think so!"

"Shit!"

Erin turned back to Rolf. The gunman appeared to be trying to do a one-armed choke hold, but the dog wasn't having any of it. The K-9's jaws only clamped tighter. No matter what the perp did to him, Rolf would hold on until Erin told him to let go. Despite the ringing in her ears from the echoing gunfire, Erin heard bone crackle. The man screamed and tried to pull away. Erin got down beside them, whipped out her cuffs, and snapped one bracelet on the guy's free hand. Then she pulled it close to the other hand, the one in the dog's mouth, and closed the other loop, cuffing him.

The guy who'd been holding the submachine-gun was down, not moving. Blood spread in a pool beneath him. She kicked the gun away and glanced back down the platform. The uniform who'd been shot was moving, she was glad to see, but he was still lying flat on his back. The other one stood by the wall in a daze.

"Hey!" she shouted at him. "Officer!"

"Huh?" He stared blankly at her.

"Get your ass over here! We got a man down and a dangerous prisoner!"

He moved, thank God. Erin wondered where their backup was. There were hundreds of cops only a few yards above them, but she had no idea when they'd start to arrive. And there was still a bomb that might or might not be armed. Did Rüdel have the detonator? Was he willing to die? If so, they'd find out any second.

Vic shared a quick look with her. "Let's do this," he growled.

"Rolf," she said. "*Pust!*"

The Shepherd immediately released his victim. Tail still wagging, he trotted to Erin's side, looking up at her expectantly. He was ready for his reward.

"*Zei brav,*" she said, telling him what a good boy he'd been.

Rolf wagged harder, agreeing that he was, indeed, a good boy.

"*Komm,*" she ordered. She, Vic, and Rolf moved toward the restroom.

"I'll go first," Vic said.

"No," she said. "I'm quicker. Cover me."

"You sure you're okay?"

Her shoulder was throbbing a little now, but it didn't seem too bad. The bullet had just caught the upper edge of her vest and she didn't see any blood. "Forget about it."

The oil-drum wires led into the bathroom, which wasn't comforting. On the other hand, the bomb hadn't blown up yet. Erin wondered again what was taking the backup so long. Then she remembered that time was weird in firefights. She'd probably find out later that they'd only been here for a minute or two.

They stacked up against the wall, Erin first, Rolf beside her, Vic bringing up the rear. Vic pulled the magazine out of his rifle, slipped in a fresh one, and chambered a round.

"Okay," he said very quietly into her ear. She felt the warmth of his breath on her ear.

Erin took a deep breath and lunged through the doorway.

Chapter 21

The only light was a faint reddish glow from an EXIT sign just over Erin's head. She saw tile walls and floors that would probably be white in daylight, but here they were stained an eerie red. Fancy sinks and faucets from an older New York lined one wall. The wires for the bombs trailed across the floor toward the back of the room. There was no sign of Rüdel.

"Rolf," she said quietly.

The dog perked his ears.

"*Fass.*"

His ears went back and he lunged into the room, following the fresh, sweaty smell of the terrorist. Rüdel might as well have left a lighted path to his location.

Erin didn't feel good about sending Rolf in, but it was the right tactical move. The dog had a vest, so unless Rüdel got lucky with a head shot, he'd probably be okay. A fast-moving dog's head was a very difficult target, especially in bad lighting.

Vic was at her back, moving into the room as Rolf hurtled toward the most distant bathroom stall. Its door was closed, but Rolf just eased his body low and slid through the eighteen-inch space at the bottom, hardly slowing down. Erin got ready for the familiar sounds of her K-9 making a collar: a snarl, the thud of a falling body, a man screaming.

Nothing happened. The dog vanished into the dark.

"The hell?" Vic wondered aloud.

Erin shook her head and followed Rolf as fast as she dared, keeping her pistol leveled in both hands. She braced herself and kicked in the stall door. Its flimsy latch snapped and the door flew open, banged into the wall, and swung shut. She shoved it open again with her left hand, keeping her Glock aimed with her right.

The side wall of the stall had a hole in it. Someone had drilled through the tile, the concrete behind it, and the dirt. It was a narrow passage, rough-cut, and led God only knew where. The bomb wires led down it, and somewhere in there was an armed killer.

But her dog was there, too, and it was her job to go in. Every second that passed gave Rüdel another chance to blow them all sky-high. From her demolitions training, she knew there were two kinds of bomb circuits; open and closed. Open-circuit wires could be safely cut. Closed-circuit wires, on the other hand, would set off the explosive if the current was interrupted. If they cut the wires, it was a coin toss whether the bomb went off or not. She hesitated. They couldn't risk it.

Up ahead, Rolf started barking.

That meant he'd run up against an obstacle he couldn't get past. Erin cursed and tried to move faster, squeezing through the dirty tunnel. She was going blind, but she thought she saw a gleam of light ahead.

A familiar stink drifted to her nose. "Great," she muttered. "More sewers." Behind her, Vic was cursing as he worked his big frame through the tunnel.

She came out into a narrow sewer passage and saw Rolf at the foot of an access ladder. The dog was leaping and scrabbling at the rungs, barking in frustration. At its base, the bomb's wires ended in a small black box with a toggle switch.

Erin raised her gun in both hands and stepped carefully to the base of the ladder, ignoring the now-harmless control box. She looked cautiously up the access shaft and saw the concrete of some sort of roof overhead.

"Erin!" Vic called. He'd gotten momentarily stuck in the tight gap. "Wait for the backup!"

She knew she should. But her instincts told her Rüdel was running. He had an escape route mapped out, she was sure of it. If she waited, they might lose their best chance at him. She could practically smell the bastard.

Erin started climbing.

She went up as quietly as she could without sacrificing speed, but the old metal ladder squeaked and creaked. When she got near the top, she found herself wondering if Rüdel would be waiting for her head to come into view. He could be standing right there.

Her heart was pounding and her mouth was dry. Would she have time to feel the impact of a bullet in the head?

"Time to find out," she whispered to herself.

She grabbed the top rung with one hand, tensed her legs, and sprang up out of the manhole shaft.

Erin had an instant to take in her surroundings. She was in the corner of some sort of basement parking garage, bare concrete with big support columns and rows of parked cars. And there, about fifteen yards in front of her, was Hans Rüdel.

He had a gun in his hands, aimed right at her.

Time slowed down. She saw his finger squeeze the trigger, saw fire blossom at the end of the barrel. The impacts came about six inches below her chin, a double-tap shot smack in the middle of her breastbone. It was like a hammer slamming into her vest. She was knocked backward and almost fell. She reflexively fired her own pistol in Rüdel's general direction.

She tried to bring her Glock back in line. Rüdel wouldn't make another body shot. He'd go for the head, and she knew he didn't miss often. Even as she raised her gun, she stared down the barrel of his weapon and knew she didn't have time.

Then Rüdel reeled sideways. Half his face vanished in a spray of blood. She heard a gunshot. Backup. On time, for once, she thought dazedly.

But Rüdel didn't go down. The shot had gone in one cheek and out the other, the exit wound tearing a big hole. It was an awful wound, but hadn't taken him out of action. The German clapped a hand to his ruined face and fired a one-handed shot at Erin, then sprayed three more bullets in the direction of the other shooter, who was somewhere to Erin's left. Then he turned and ran.

Time went into slow motion again.

A question a lot of cops had to ask themselves was whether they'd shoot a running criminal in the back. Usually the answer was "no." The NYPD's guidelines were, "Police officers shall not use deadly physical force against another person unless they have probable cause to believe they must protect themselves or another person present from imminent death or serious physical injury." Erin had memorized that phrase. She'd also shot and killed a man earlier that summer, and sometimes she still woke up in a cold sweat thinking about that moment.

"Drop it, Rüdel!" she screamed. "NYPD!"

His only answer was two more blind shots over his shoulder.

Erin lined up the Glock's sights. Rüdel was running toward a black Ford Taurus a few yards away. He was about three strides from it when she fired.

She aimed center mass, two quick shots, like she'd practiced. The bullets punched into Rüdel's back just a little left of his spine. Even as Erin shifted aim for the head, he stumbled and slammed into the side of the car, losing his grip on his gun. It skittered across the roof of the car and vanished from view.

Erin started running toward him. He was badly wounded, probably incapacitated, and disarmed. She could take him alive, and in spite of everything he'd done and tried to do, that was what she wanted.

"Get down, lass!" a female voice shouted in a strangely familiar accent. Erin faltered and came to a halt, trying to think where she'd heard that voice. But she didn't take her eyes off Rüdel.

In that moment of hesitation, he fumbled a car key out of his pocket with bloody fingers. He yanked the sedan's door open and fell inside.

Then Erin realized what was going to happen. She dove for the floor as Rüdel shoved the key into the ignition and twisted it.

The car exploded.

One second the vehicle was there, the next an expanding fireball swallowed it and vomited out a cloud of spinning debris. Every windshield and window in the row of parked cars shattered. A car door tumbled end over end right at Erin, passing over her by less than two feet and crashing against the wall of the garage. The heat on her face was like an open oven door. She squeezed her eyes shut and buried her head in her arms, curling into a protective ball. Temporarily deafened, she felt rather than heard the clatter of twisted chunks of Detroit steel as they rained down on all sides.

She lay there, stunned, tasting gritty concrete dust and blood. Her nose was bleeding and she felt like hammers were beating the inside of her skull. She realized she was feeling her own heartbeat. That meant she wasn't dead. That was comforting.

Faintly, echoing, she heard someone shouting.

"Erin! Erin!"

Her lips formed the word "Vic." She wasn't sure if she said it or not. Her thoughts were slow and muddled.

Then he was there, holding her by the shoulders. She made her eyes focus on his face. She'd never seen him look so scared.

"Where are you hurt?" he was asking.

She shook her head. "I'm okay," she slurred. "I didn't think you cared."

He laughed in a way that would've been hysterical in anyone less tough than Vic Neshenko. "Holy shit, girl. What the hell happened?"

"Check the other officer," she said. Her hearing was starting to come back, a little. She sat up.

"What other officer?"

"Backup. Shot Rüdel."

Vic stood and looked around the garage. "There's no one else here, Erin."

She shook her head again. "No. A woman... Good shot." Then her brain caught up with her mouth and she got quiet.

"Erin," Vic said. "You want to start explaining?"

Sirens were blaring outside the garage. Of course, Erin thought. Hundreds of cops. Police headquarters was right there, after all. They'd probably been able to see the smoke from the front door.

"Rüdel's dead," she told Vic.

"You get him?"

"Yes. No. I don't know."

"But you know he's dead. For a fact."

"Yeah." Erin pointed to the wreckage of the Taurus. Some of it was still burning. "That's him."

"Jesus Christ," Vic said. "When you take a guy out, you don't screw around."

The first squad car screamed down the garage ramp and squealed to a halt. Vic held up his shield as cops spilled out of it. "Take it easy," he said to Erin. "It's over."

Chapter 22

"You sure about this?" Webb asked.

Erin was sick of being asked that. "Yeah. It was Siobhan."

"What was she doing here?"

Erin shrugged. "Killing Rüdel."

Webb sighed. "Okay, tell me again."

She and Vic went over things one more time. They were standing in the garage, surrounded by police. Skip Taylor and the Bomb Squad were sniffing around the smoking wreckage of the Taurus. An ESU medic had just finished looking Erin over and pronounced her healthy, more or less. She had a couple of bad bruises from the bullets that had hit her vest, but the nosebleed and tinnitus from the bomb blast were largely superficial. She was otherwise fine. Vic and Rolf didn't have a scratch on them. Erin had helped a couple of ESU guys hoist the dog up the sewer ladder with one of their fast-ropes. The K-9 was lying on the ground beside her, gnawing contentedly on his chew-toy.

The press conference was going on about two hundred yards south of them. The Commissioner was in the process of announcing that Hans Rüdel, terrorist, had died in an explosion, apparently self-inflicted. Erin had just told Webb that wasn't the truth.

"Siobhan knew his car from the rental computer," she finished. "She waited until the coast was clear, then wired a bomb to the ignition. After that, she set up a spot where she could watch."

"Why not just walk away?" Webb asked.

"She had to be sure of the kill," Erin replied. "What if one of Rüdel's guys got in the car instead of him? She set up a sniper spot, I guess in her car."

"I saw a car leaving," Vic said. "Right after the explosion. I got up the ladder just in time to see it pull out. I called in the make and model. Honda Civic, silver. Didn't catch the plate. Good luck finding that. There's gotta be hundreds of 'em in this city."

"But neither of you actually saw Finneran?" Webb asked.

"Like I said, I heard her," Erin said. "She yelled at me to get down."

"Why'd she do that?" Vic wondered.

Erin shrugged again. "I'm glad she did. She saved my life."

"So we're looking for an assassin who came here from Ireland for the purpose of killing a terrorist," Webb said. "One who risked being ID'd in order to protect a cop."

"That you'd already shot," Vic added, nodding to Erin. "You think it was a kill shot?"

"Yeah. I hit him twice, center mass."

"So Finneran killed a guy who was already gonna die," Vic said. "What's that mean?"

"It means she committed murder one," Webb said. "Doesn't matter what happened before that. And she planted a big goddamn explosive device in a Manhattan parking garage. So this was a public-service homicide. Doesn't keep it from being a homicide." He paused. "You were right about the car, by the way. Jones called it in about the time it blew up. A skinhead type rented a black Taurus. The clerk remembered Finneran, and Jones has the skinhead on tape."

"Ten bucks says it's one of the guys we got in the subway," Vic said.

"No bet," Erin said. "Damn. If we'd gotten that tip an hour earlier..."

"Wouldn't have mattered," Vic said. "We couldn't have found a car that common fast enough."

"How'd your anonymous tipster know about the subway, anyway?" Webb asked.

"You'd have to ask him," she said.

"I'll do that," Webb said. "If I ever meet him. But I'm sure it's occurred to you that this anonymous source might be affiliated with Rüdel."

"He's not," Erin said firmly.

"So you know who he is," Webb said.

She sometimes forgot her CO was a detective, and a damn good one. "I can't bring him into this," she said. "He's a valuable CI. Without him, we'd have lost a couple hundred people today, minimum. We owe him his privacy."

Webb nodded reluctantly. "We'll play it your way, for now. But sooner or later, someone's gonna want to know who that was."

"What's the status on our wounded cop?" Vic asked. "And the two mopes in the station?"

"Our guy's got a bullet in his leg, a broken jaw, and a concussion," Webb said. "Serious condition, but he's gonna pull through. He took one in the face, but the medic says it hitting the jaw was good. The bone absorbed most of the force. The concussion's from hitting his head on the floor."

"And the bad guys?" Erin asked.

"One dead, one injured," Webb replied. "The dead guy caught three rifle rounds dead center. Good shooting, Neshenko."

Vic snorted. "I fired half a clip at him. I should've hit more than three times."

"In the dark," Erin reminded him.

"Whatever."

"The injured guy has both bones in his right arm broken," Webb continued. "And some bad-ass tooth marks."

"I keep telling Erin, she's gotta stop biting the perps," Vic said. "It's a liability issue."

"Who were they?" Erin asked.

"Out-of-towners," Webb said. "They flew in to La Guardia on false passports from Frankfurt. That's when they rented the car, probably. Once we ID them, I'm guessing we'll find out they're on Homeland's watch list. The Homeland guys are pissed they managed to get into the country at all."

"What do we do now?" Vic asked.

"Go home, shower, and change into your dress blues," Webb said. "Try not to talk to any reporters on the way."

"Dress blues?" Vic echoed. "The hell for? They're not giving us a medal, are they?"

"They will eventually," Webb said. "But now, you've got a departmental funeral to attend. So do I. Taylor and his boys will work this site with CSU."

"What about Siobhan?" Erin asked.

"If we were going to catch her today, we'd have done it already," Webb said. "Unless you think she's sticking around?"

Erin thought about it and shook her head. "She's probably already out of Manhattan. But we should put out a BOLO."

"We'll do that," Webb said. "But she's sure to have an exit lined up. Besides, you think we'll find anything but circumstantial evidence to tie her to this?"

"I hate professional hitmen," Vic growled. "Hitwomen. Whatever."

"You're just pissed you didn't get to shoot Rüdel again," Erin said.

"For the love of God, don't say that in front of a reporter," Webb said. "You can tackle the paperwork after the funeral," he added.

"Oh, God," Vic said. "You think they'd bury me, too, if I asked them?"

*   *   *

Back at her apartment, Erin stripped off her filthy clothes and climbed into the shower. The smell of smoke, dirty water, and subway grime clung to her. Even after two doses of shampoo, she could still smell it. Rolf needed a bath, badly, but there wasn't time. He wouldn't be attending the funeral in any case.

She put on her dress uniform and some basic makeup. While she applied her mascara, she caught a glimpse at her eyes. The hollow look in them shook her so badly she smeared a dark streak across her cheek by accident. She managed to finish applying the makeup without meeting her own gaze again.

She didn't like the stiff black shoes and white gloves. She especially didn't like not wearing a gun, but a holster wasn't worn over the NYPD dress jacket. Besides, her sidearm was in the possession of Internal Affairs, since it had just been used in an officer-involved shooting. But Erin didn't intend to be totally defenseless, not even at a funeral full of cops. Her backup gun, a snub-nosed revolver, fit nicely in an ankle holster under her uniform trousers. The white gloves and her police hat completed the ensemble.

Erin was afraid if she stopped moving and started thinking, she might come apart. She was exhausted. Her bruises hurt. If she closed her eyes, she could still see down the muzzle of Rüdel's gun and watch the car door hurtle through the space she'd been standing in a second before. The very last thing she wanted to do was to be reminded of her own mortality. But Hendricks had been one of their own. She had to be there.

The service was at St. Patrick's Cathedral in Manhattan. Erin stepped into a sea of blue uniforms and grim, serious faces. She worked her way through the crowd until she recognized some faces from Precinct 8.

"Captain," she called.

Captain Holliday nodded to her. "Thanks for coming, Detective. I understand you've had a busy day. Good work out there."

"Thank you, sir."

"Erin," Kira said from a little behind the Captain. "You okay?"

"Yeah. Is Vic here?"

"I saw him a minute ago," Kira said. "He's around, somewhere."

Then Erin saw him, looking uptight and uncomfortable. She realized it was the first time she'd seen him in uniform. It didn't suit him at all.

There wasn't room in the church for all the officers. Erin and her squadmates entered, removed their hats, and stood at attention, waiting.

They waited a while. Eventually, the flag team came in, followed by the pallbearers. There was some sort of brief confusion at the door. Erin's five-foot-six build wasn't tall enough to see what was going on, but things quickly got sorted out. Then the half-dozen pallbearers came down the aisle carrying Hendricks's casket.

A bagpipe started playing "Amazing Grace." Erin reflected that, when an officer joined the NYPD, they were granted a sort of honorary Celtic ethnicity. She watched five men and one woman carrying Officer Hendricks to the altar and felt an unexpected lump in her throat. She'd hardly known the rookie, but he'd been one of their own. She remembered John Brunanski. She'd held his hand while he died.

Erin heard muffled sniffles from some of the men around her. That was fine for them. It was a great time for manly tears. But she didn't feel like she could show that kind of emotion. From her, it might be taken as feminine weakness. So she gritted her teeth and stared straight ahead, keeping her jaw firm and her chin high.

The Archbishop of New York took his place at the front and started the service with his invocation. Erin didn't even register his words. Something was tugging at her memory, something a little out of place. There was a brief prayer, a murmured chorus of "amen" from the assembled officers, and they sat down.

Erin was thinking about the honor guard. One of the pallbearers had caught her eye. It'd been the middle guy on the right. His face had looked different from the others. They'd all been holding that stoic self-control she knew was on her own face, but that guy was more in command of himself. He'd looked like a cop just doing his job, as if he'd been talking to a civilian about a fatal car crash. He'd had no personal investment in the situation, and that was pretty damn weird in a pallbearer.

Then she realized why that must be. He was a substitute. One of the original pallbearers hadn't been able to go through with it. That wasn't unheard of. It was an emotional thing for any officer, and those six would've been the officers closest to Hendricks.

She knew immediately who was missing. His partner, Bob Michaelson.

The opening remarks had ended. A young woman, not in uniform, came forward. She began singing "Ave Maria" in a high, clear soprano voice. Erin heard more sniffling. To her surprise, she saw Vic surreptitiously wipe at his eyes. She wondered who the woman was. Wife? Sister? She realized she'd forgotten to get her hands on a program.

Her thoughts went back to Michaelson. He should've been there. Yeah, he was upset. Yeah, she was planning on arresting him for murder. That didn't matter. This was one duty no cop was allowed to shirk. When your partner got killed, you came to the damn funeral. That was the rules.

The archbishop was reading a scripture verse now. It was a classic.

"This is my commandment: love one another as I love you. No one has greater love than this, to lay down one's life for one's friends. You are my friends if you do what I command you. I no longer call you slaves, because a slave does not know what his master is doing. I have called you friends, because I have told you everything I have heard from my Father. It was not you who chose me, but I who chose you and appointed you to go and bear fruit that will remain, so that whatever you ask the Father in my name he may give you. This I command you: love one another."

Damn it, where was Michaelson?

"Oh, God," Vic murmured very quietly. It didn't sound like a prayer. Erin could sympathize with him. The Mayor was getting up to say a few words. It was supposed to be respectful, and Erin supposed it was, but she also knew she wouldn't want any elected official saying anything at her funeral, no matter what his politics were.

She zoned out the service. It was hard to keep her focus anyway. The rest of it was a blur; the eulogy, some more music, the closing remarks and another prayer. Then they were standing at attention again and the bagpiper went back to work. The pipes died away into silence. They stayed standing.

An officer went to the mike. Over the church's speakers came his voice.

"Dispatch calling Twelve Juliet... Twelve Juliet... Dispatch calling Officer Randall Hendricks, shield nine three six three. No answer Twelve Juliet. Twelve Juliet out of service. Gone but not forgotten."

Erin's self-control wasn't up to the task in the end. She watched the casket carried out of the church through a veil of tears.

Chapter 23

The police officers stood and filed out in disciplined silence. Erin wiped her eyes, cleared her throat, and tried to look firm and professional. She knew what would be waiting for them outside.

Sure enough, behind the ranks of assembled NYPD uniforms were the reporters, photographers, and cameramen. Flashbulbs went off on all sides of them, and for a nightmarish instant Erin was back in the subway station, watching muzzle flashes and hearing gunfire.

Another officer nudged her with an elbow. She came back to the present and kept walking, her thoughts spinning. She was trying to think about Michaelson; how he'd looked at their last interview, what he was feeling, what he'd do.

He was dirty, she knew that. He'd been taking money from Tommy Jay O'Malley, and in addition to whatever information he'd passed on, he'd committed murder on behalf of the Mob. But the main question right now was, what did that have to do with Hendricks?

Tommy Jay had hidden Rüdel. He'd given the German access to building plans, info about explosives in an O'Malley warehouse, maybe weapons and medical attention. But at the same time, Evan O'Malley had brought in Siobhan Finneran specifically to kill Rüdel. Maybe Tommy Jay had experienced a change of heart, or maybe he'd just bowed to pressure from his boss. Regardless, if he was trying to clean up his mess, what would he do?

He'd send a hitman to take care of Rüdel. And what better asset than his man in the NYPD? All Tommy Jay had to do was tell Rüdel to hit a particular warehouse, at a particular time, and then tip off Michaelson.

Which meant Michaelson didn't just feel guilty about Hendricks getting killed because they'd been partners. It meant he felt directly responsible for putting the rookie in the line of fire.

"Shit," Erin muttered.

"What's the problem, O'Reilly?" Webb asked.

"We have to go."

"To the cemetery," he agreed.

"No. We gotta get to Michaelson."

"There's time for that later."

"No, sir, there isn't."

Webb wasn't happy. "This can wait."

"I don't think it can."

"Look, O'Reilly, you've done plenty for one day. What's your problem?"

She stopped and turned to face him. They were disrupting the line of march, but she didn't care. "He may not be around later. He thinks this whole thing is his fault."

Webb got it, a little. "Okay, I'll call a unit, have them drop by his place."

"Not good enough, sir."

"Do you have to do everything yourself?"

"I have to do this."

"What's the holdup back there?" Captain Holliday called down the line.

"Okay," Webb said. "But take someone with you."

"I'll go," Kira said.

"Me too," Vic said.

"Not you, Neshenko," Webb said. "It sounds like this may call for a more delicate touch. You're not exactly our best negotiator. You two, go."

The two women slipped out of the line of officers and into the crowd. Several heads turned to watch them go, but no one said anything. Police were used to being suddenly called away.

"Why are you so eager for this?" Erin asked as they worked their way toward her car.

"I missed the thing at One PP," Kira said. "Geez, I let you guys down. I could've moved faster."

"Not your fault," Erin said. "You were doing your job."

"About that..."

"What?"

Kira dropped her eyes to one side. "Forget about it. I'll tell you after."

Erin was parked in a police spot four blocks south and two east of the cathedral; the closest she'd been able to get, and better than she'd dared hope, given all the police cars. But she was very aware of the time it was taking them to walk. She sped up to a jog.

"Why aren't you letting a local unit handle it?" Kira asked, keeping pace beside her.

"They won't understand, and there's no time to explain."

"We've got the road stopped up for the funeral procession," Kira said. "It's gonna screw with traffic patterns all over the place."

"We'll use the siren till we're free of the jam."

They got into Erin's Charger. She started it rolling, peeling off her white gloves as she drove. She dropped her hat beside the seat.

"So what do you think?" Kira asked. "He skipping town?"

Erin shook her head. "I think he's in danger. From himself."

*   *   *

The lobby of Michaelson's apartment building was empty except for an elderly man reading a newspaper. He cocked an eyebrow through the glass doors at the two dress-uniformed detectives, but didn't say anything as Erin pushed the buzzer for Michaelson's unit.

There was no answer.

She waited a few seconds and tried again, with the same result.

She buzzed him one more time, holding down the intercom button. "Hey, Bob. Let us in, okay? It's O'Reilly. I just want to talk, see how you're doing." She paused. "You up there, man? Come on."

Kira waved to the old gentleman and showed him her shield. He stood up, shuffled slowly to the door, and opened it.

"Good afternoon, miss," he said, touching a fingertip to his forehead politely. "How may I be of service?"

"That'll do fine, sir," Erin said, squeezing past him and running to the elevator. Kira caught up to her while she was waiting for the doors to open.

"I'm not armed, you know," Kira said in a calm, conversational tone as the car rose toward the fourth floor. "We arresting him?"

"Maybe." Erin knelt and drew her holdout revolver, checking the cylinder. She slipped the pistol into her pocket within easier reach.

"That's not gonna go over well with the Department," Kira said. "Taking a guy in on the day of his partner's funeral?"

Erin didn't answer. The elevator bell chimed and the doors slid open.

She knocked on Michaelson's door. "Hey, Bob!" she called. "Could you open up? We have to talk."

More silence greeted her.

"You think he's here?" Kira asked. Her eyes widened. "Shit, you don't think he already—"

"No."

"How do you know?"

"No one reported a gunshot." Erin wished she was as confident as she sounded. She was looking at the door and thinking. They couldn't legally enter without probable cause. Breaking down that door would be a major infraction.

She leaned in close. "Hey, Bob! I got a report of a 10-13 from this location. You okay in there?"

"Erin, what are you doing?" Kira hissed. "There wasn't a call and you know it!"

"There's a cop in there who needs help," Erin said through clenched teeth.

"I didn't think you came here to help him."

Erin gave her a look. "That's exactly what I came for." She tried the doorknob.

It wasn't locked. She was thrilled, for a second. Then the door swung in two inches and stopped, held back by the chain of the night-lock. Erin took a breath and kicked the door open.

A chain lock wasn't a sturdy barrier. The thin metal links snapped with a musical clink and the door flew open. Erin went in, remembering the layout of the apartment. She checked the kitchen and living room, finding them empty. Kira was standing in the entryway at a loss for what to do.

"Bedroom," Erin said, leading the way down the short hall. She rounded the corner and stepped through the doorway.

Bob Michaelson sat on the foot of his bed. His service sidearm was in his hand, a Glock just like Erin's. Its barrel was aimed at the side of his own head. He looked up at the two women through bloodshot eyes.

Erin pulled her revolver and threw down on him reflexively, thinking what a stupid thing it was to do. What was she going to do, shoot him if he shot himself? But their training was clear on the subject. A guy with a gun was dangerous. He might decide to shoot them instead.

"Whoa there, Bob," she said, keeping her voice as calm as possible. "What's going on here?"

"Just taking care of something," he said. His voice was as flat and dead as anything she'd ever heard.

Erin wished she'd brought a hostage negotiator with her. She tried to remember all the rules. Don't ever say "no." Don't cut off options. Keep talking, keep listening. Get him to open up.

"Talk to me, man," she said. She lowered the muzzle of her gun a little. "I know you're hurting. This is a 10-13, Bob. You need help. I've got your back."

He shook his head. "No. I'm not gonna pull any more shields into this."

"Don't worry about us, Bob," she said. "We're here for you."

A tear rolled down Michaelson's cheek. "You don't know."

"Yeah, we do," Erin said. "We know Tommy Jay told you where to find Rüdel."

"You do?"

She nodded. "It'll be okay, Bob." She took a step into the room, just a small one. "You're a good cop."

"No, I'm not."

"The hell you're not," she said. "You've been trying to do the right thing. Hell, you're still trying. But you're a little confused is all. You want to punish the bad guy, right?"

His eyes darted sidelong at the pistol in his hand. Erin cursed inwardly. A negotiator wasn't supposed to remind the guy with the gun that he wanted to die.

"Thing is," she went on quickly, "you're not the bad guy here. Rüdel was a bad guy. And Tommy Jay is a bad guy. You want someone to go down for this, why not them?"

Michaelson shook his head. "You don't get it. I've done some bad shit."

"Carl told me," Erin said quietly, taking another step. She was about six feet away. It was almost close enough for a quick lunge, but that would be a huge risk.

"You talked to Carl?" Michaelson asked, meeting her eyes for the first time. "How is he?"

"He's okay," she lied. "It's eating him up, though. What happened with those Colombians. He feels guilty, like it was his fault."

"It wasn't!" Michaelson snapped. There was definitely a spark of life in him now. Erin didn't know if that was a good thing or not. "He didn't have anything to do with it!"

"I know," she said. "But someone needs to stand up and say that. You've got to tell the truth, Bob. You've got to be alive for that. Carl needs you. And so do we."

The Glock's barrel wavered.

"Hendricks didn't stay in the car," Michaelson said softly. More tears were in his eyes. "I told him to stay in the car. But he wanted the collar. He wanted to be a goddamn hero. We should've waited, called for ESU."

"We stopped Rüdel," Erin said. "He didn't kill anyone else. It's gonna be okay, Bob."

"They'll throw me in prison," he said miserably. "You know what happens to cops there."

"We can protect you," she said, risking one more step. "You're the only one who can give us Thomas O'Malley. You've got leverage. You can make a good deal."

"It was so easy," Michaelson whispered. "You've got no idea how easy it is, at first. Then when it gets hard, there's no way out and you're stuck. You get on the train and you've gotta ride it all the way to the end of the line. The end of the line," he repeated.

Erin saw his hand tighten on the grip of the gun. She saw the sudden determination in his face. Without hesitation, she dove forward and grabbed his hand, twisting it up and back.

The gunshot was tremendously loud. Plaster dust rained down from the ceiling. Michaelson was struggling with her. He was a big guy, a little overweight, half again Erin's size. In another second he might have pulled free, but Kira was there, too. Between them they wrestled the gun out of his hand. Erin kicked it across the bedroom floor.

All the fight went out of Michaelson. He collapsed against Erin, burying his head on her shoulder. It was the first time she'd had to arrest someone who was crying in her arms. She didn't know quite how to handle it.

What she said was, "It'll be okay, Bob." But she knew it wouldn't be.

Chapter 24

"Detectives," Lieutenant Keane said. "We need to talk."

Erin had known this was coming ever since they'd brought in Michaelson. They could hardly arrest a cop without hearing from Internal Affairs. She, Kira, and Rolf were in the observation room next door to Interrogation, watching Michaelson write out his statement. His lawyer and union rep were in there with him. The only thing about Keane's arrival that surprised her was that it had taken him so long to turn up.

"Lieutenant," Kira said, coming to attention.

Erin was too tired to go through the formalities. "Sir," she said with a slight nod.

The Bloodhound smiled at them with his mouth, but not with his eyes. "I understand you've brought in one of ours."

Kira glanced at Erin, who said nothing. "Yes, sir," Kira said.

"I wasn't aware we had Officer Michaelson under investigation. A paperwork oversight, maybe."

Erin turned to face him. "With respect, sir, why not cut the bullshit?"

Keane's smile sharpened on his lean, angular face. "I'd love to hear your explanation, Detective."

"There was an active investigation, and you know it, because you were running it."

It was Keane's turn to wait silently.

"You were just looking at the wrong cop," Erin went on.

Keane's eyes drifted to Kira. "I wonder what gave you that idea."

"It made sense," Erin said. "I'd helped out the O'Malleys a couple times, pretty much by accident. It was starting to look like a pattern. And there really was a mole in the department. Michaelson killed two Colombian cartel members eight years back, on orders from the O'Malleys."

"You have a firm case here?" Keane asked.

"He already confessed. He's writing it down now. And we've got his partner's testimony. The DA's gonna offer Michaelson a deal if he flips on O'Malley."

"I very much doubt he can give you Evan O'Malley," Keane said.

"Different O'Malley," Erin said. "Tommy Jay."

"Ah."

"Michaelson's looking at eight to ten, with protection while he's inside," Kira said. "It's the best deal he's going to get, under the circumstances."

Keane nodded. "You two did this as, what, a side project?"

"That's right, sir," Erin said.

"While you were chasing down a terrorist?"

They nodded.

"I have to say, I'm impressed. This is remarkable." Keane turned to look through the one-way mirror at Michaelson. "You should consider coming to work for me."

"I've already got a job, sir," Erin said.

He chuckled quietly. "I know what they say about us. We're the enemies of real cops. We're pencil-pushers who don't understand the boots on the ground. But you've already been doing our work, Detective. And without us, what's to keep the police from doing whatever the hell they want? We're the ones who watch the watchmen. And if it's your career you're worried about, IAB can offer a fine path to the upper echelons of the NYPD."

"You're serious?" Erin scoffed.

He turned back to her. "Do I look like I'm joking?"

She couldn't read him at all. He had one hell of a poker face. "Couldn't say, sir."

"You already know my answer," Kira said.

"Yes," Keane said. "And thank you."

Erin spun toward her fellow detective. "Kira? What's he talking about?"

"It's what I was going to tell you earlier," Kira said. "You're right. Major Crimes isn't the place for me. I can't do it anymore."

"The hell you can't! You've done everything you had to, every step of the way. You had my back with the Russians last summer. You're a hell of a researcher. You know every goddamn page of the Patrol Guide. You're a great cop!"

Kira shook her head. "I just can't, Erin. Every time I go out there, I'm scared to death. I hardly sleep anymore. I keep a gun under my pillow, you know that? Some day I'm gonna wake up screaming, grab it, and waste some poor bastard in the next apartment. I've got to get my head on straight. I need to work a desk for a while, crunch numbers, build cases without kicking doors. If that makes me a coward, maybe I'm a damn coward."

"If you were a coward," Erin said softly, "you wouldn't have gone in when you were scared. You're braver than I am."

Kira laughed shakily. "No way, girl. You? You're crazy." She paused. "I put in my transfer papers already."

"And we're glad to have you," Keane said. "Detective O'Reilly, my offer is still open. If you ever need a place to go, you know where to find me."

Erin considered telling him what he could do with his offer, but figured it wasn't good politics to say so. "Thanks," was what she said.

"Internal Affairs will, of course, be taking over this case," Keane said. "Since it involves an officer who has confessed to a major felony. O'Reilly, it looks like we don't require you at the moment. Jones, you and I have some things to discuss."

Erin held on to her poker face. "You can have it," she said. "Sir." She turned to go.

"One more thing, Detective," Keane said as she reached for the doorknob. "Have you considered all the ramifications of your actions? Burning Thomas O'Malley will shake up the leadership of the O'Malleys. From what I know of that organization, the succession isn't entirely clear. I suspect some of the other middle management may find their situations somewhat improved by his fall. From the sound of things, I'd be surprised if your associate Morton Carlyle wasn't promoted to Evan O'Malley's second-in-command."

"Good for him," Erin said without turning. She left the room.

She wanted nothing more than to get out of the precinct, but she couldn't leave yet. There was a biblical amount of paperwork waiting for her in Major Crimes. She had to go through Booking to get there. As she led Rolf past the desk, she was aware of a hush in the other officers' conversations. She caught little snatches of sentences behind her back.

"...busted Bob Michaelson..."

"...probably with IAB the whole time..."

"...always looking for the big collars..."

"...angling for Lieutenant..."

"...bet I know how she made Second Grade so fast..."

The rumor mill was churning away. Erin ground her teeth, but she ignored the whispers and went upstairs.

Hours later, it was after nine o'clock. She'd skipped dinner, but she was mostly done processing her share of the forms and reports from both incidents. Vic had done his part, but he'd only had to write up the Police Headquarters attack. He'd left two hours before, leaving her and Rolf alone in Major Crimes. Her wrists, fingers, and head ached. She needed a drink worse than any time she could remember.

"Okay, boy," she said to Rolf. "Let's go home."

She almost made it out of the precinct unnoticed. She was halfway down the corridor to the parking garage and already imagining how good her shower was going to feel.

"Erin!"

Her spine stiffened involuntarily. Then she recognized the voice and turned, trying to muster a smile. "Skip."

The bomb tech jogged up behind her. "Glad I caught you. I've got something on the car bomb."

"Yeah?" It was hard to be enthusiastic at the moment.

"It'll be a while before we finish putting it all together," he said. "But you need to hear this. That bomb wasn't a suicide device."

"I know."

"I mean it!" he insisted. "Someone planted the bomb to kill the victim. This is a homicide, no doubt about it."

"Skip, I know."

"Huh? How?"

She sighed. "Never mind. Put it in your report, and I'll look at it in the morning. Is that all you got?"

Skip deflated a little, but he rallied. "There's something else. I recognize the signature of the device."

"You do?"

"Yeah. It's a classic IRA car bomb. Ammonium nitrate fuel oil. Like the ones they used in Belfast in the early '90s to hit British Army checkpoints."

"So?"

"So the bomber was trained by the IRA. I'm, like, ninety percent sure."

"Skip?"

He stopped talking and looked at her.

"Skip, *I know*."

He spread his hands. "Then what the hell have I been doing all afternoon?"

She wanted to say, "Wasting your time." But that would've been mean-spirited and not quite true. "Building a case," she said. "In case the bomber ever comes back to town."

"I thought maybe it was a guy who lived here," he said. "The bomb reminded me of—"

"It wasn't Carlyle," she said sharply.

"Erin, how do you know?"

"I know who set the bomb. It was Siobhan Finneran. She warned me right before it went off. And she's gone."

"Can you prove it?"

"That's what you're gonna help with, Skip," she said. "Get anything we can use, write it up, send me your report, and I'll look at it. In the morning." She tried to go a little easier on him. She liked Skip. "And thanks, man. Any hard evidence you can give us will be a help."

"I'll see what I can do." He looked at her a little more closely. "You good?"

"I'm good, Skip. I just need some rest."

*   *   *

Back home, she took off her dress uniform. It would definitely need a trip to the dry-cleaner. After stripping down to her underwear, she gave Rolf the scrubbing he desperately needed. She toweled him off and fed him. Then it was her turn to step into the shower for the second time that day. She couldn't decide whether to collapse or to bounce off the walls. She was exhausted, wired, angry, exhilarated, and sore. The bullet impacts on her chest had left spectacular bruises on her sternum and the inner part of her shoulder. She hardly cared. She put on a pair of sweatpants and an NYPD sweatshirt and left the bathroom.

Now that she was finally away from the Job, with a chance to let go of it and relax, that was the very last thing she was able to do. The whole day replayed itself in her head, going into slow motion for the best parts, like the car exploding in front of her and lying on her stomach in the subway station watching bullets kick concrete chips into her face.

She'd get that drink, Erin decided. She changed clothes for what felt like the hundredth time since she'd woken up, into black slacks and a navy blouse. Her hair was still wet, and she wasn't about to do anything fancy with it, so it went into a ponytail. Rolf, lying on the bed, watched her with his face between his paws.

"I'll be back," she promised. "You just take it easy."

He obediently stayed where he was. And Erin went to see a friend about that drink.

Chapter 25

The Barley Corner's evening crowd was as big as ever. The atmosphere was more relaxed than the last time she'd been there. News had clearly tricked down about the events at One PP.

Erin went straight for the bar, whiskey on her mind. Carlyle was there, on his stool, leaning against the bar and watching the room. He was dressed with his usual care, charcoal coat over gray silk shirt, neatly knotted black necktie. He saw her at the same moment she saw him, and the look that was in his eyes was pure relief. Then he hid the emotion behind his game face, the pleasant smile that gave nothing away.

"Evening, Erin," he said, standing to greet her. He looked at her more closely, with a hint of concern now. "Are you well, darling?"

"I need a goddamn drink," she said. "And we need to talk."

"Aye, perhaps we do," he said. "But I'm thinking this may not be the place to do it. If you'd care to step upstairs, I've a private bottle you might find agreeable."

"Keep the good stuff for yourself, do you?"

"If that were the case, I'd hardly be sharing it."

"Okay, let's see what you've got."

Up in Carlyle's suite, she took a seat on his couch while he opened his cabinet. "What's your pleasure?" he asked.

"Just not another damn cocktail," she said. "You're giving me a drink, I want to taste the alcohol."

"I've just the thing," he said. He came back with two glasses and a bottle of Glen Docherty-Kinlochewe whiskey.

"I've ice if you're wanting it," he said.

"Straight up," Erin said.

"Just my thinking." He took a seat beside her and poured. They drank.

Carlyle waited, watching her, taking small sips from his glass. She finished her first shot and held out her glass for another.

"Two-drink day?" he asked, pouring her refill.

"Twenty-two drinks might be more like it."

"I've seen the news reports," he said. "That bad, then?"

"I ran into your girl."

He nodded. "I know it."

"Have you seen her?"

"Nay. She telephoned me."

"From where?"

He shook his head. "You'll not catch her, Erin. Not today. She's well quit of New York by now." He took another sip of whiskey and sighed. "I know you did your best to do what I asked, and I appreciate it."

"Siobhan would've got Rüdel one way or another," Erin said. "You taught her too damn well."

"But he'd have accomplished his aim first," he said. "If not for you."

"What do you care if a bunch of cops get killed?"

He put down his half-empty shot glass. "Erin, I'm no monster. I've no wish to see innocent men and women die."

"Unless it's good for business?"

"The death of innocents is never good business."

Erin finished her second whiskey. The pounding in her head was gone. She was actually feeling a little better. "We wouldn't have gotten there in time without you," she said. "So... thanks."

"I'm glad I could help."

"So is this another favor I owe you?"

Carlyle winced. "I'd rather hoped we were past all that."

"You told me once that the world runs on favors."

"Aye, so it does."

"But then again," she said, "once we bust your buddy Tommy Jay, that ought to even us up. Is that why you did it?"

"Arrest Thomas?" Carlyle seemed startled by the idea. "What has he done?"

"There was that time he tried to have you killed," she reminded him.

He smiled. "Very well. What can you prove that he's done?"

"He had a dirty cop whack a couple rival drug dealers a few years back."

Carlyle nodded. "I see. Well, I'll not take credit for any case you've managed to make. That's your good police work, and perhaps a bit of carelessness on his part."

"I shouldn't even be telling you this," she said. "We haven't picked him up yet. But somehow, I don't think you'll be calling him to tip him off."

He smiled. "Nay, your secret's in the best of hands. I've no love for the man. He's made his bed, and he's the one will have to lie in it."

"And you get promoted."

"Does it trouble you if that's so?"

She had to think about that. "I don't know," she said after a moment. "You're a criminal, Carlyle."

"And?"

She looked him straight in the eye. "And I don't know why."

"You know my history," he said. "You've read the file the Brits have on me. You know where I come from."

"Yeah, but you could've done something else. When you came to America, why'd you fall in with Evan O'Malley?"

Carlyle bought himself some time finishing his whiskey. He held the empty glass for a moment, staring into it, remembering.

"I've told you of Rose McCann," he said at last.

"Your wife, yeah."

"The Ulster Volunteer Force killed her," he said. "With bloody machine guns, in our flat. I've always suspected they were trying for me, but I've no proof of it. It might have been simple terrorism. They did that, you ken. Just killed Catholic civilians, for the sake of fear alone. The heart went out of me when they did that. I couldn't help seeing the whole terrible wastefulness of it all. I suppose they killed my idealism that day. I couldn't very well keep working for the Brigades. I couldn't stand the thought of Ireland, even. I had to get away from that place."

"I thought you loved Ireland," Erin said.

"So I do, for what she gave me. And I hate her as well, for what she took from me. When I came here, I'd no prospects, no plans nor intentions. I'd a hole in me that Evan offered me the chance to fill."

"Do you still miss her?" Erin asked.

"Ireland? Or Rosie? Oh, aye. You've never been married, have you?"

"Me?" She couldn't help laughing. "No. The Job doesn't really allow for that sort of thing."

"That's nonsense," Carlyle said. "There's many a copper with a family."

She nodded. "Maybe it's me, then. There was this guy, earlier this year... He was a good guy, sweet, fun to be around. But he was a civvie, and the Job scared him off. Since then? I wonder whether anyone who's not in the Job can really get close to someone who is. Civilians just don't get it."

"So you're looking for another copper, then?"

"God, no! That's the last thing I need!"

Carlyle smiled. "Then I'm afraid there's only two choices left you."

"I can die an old maid," she said, smiling back. "That what Mom's afraid of. There's another choice?"

"You can find yourself a gangster."

She almost laughed. Then she saw the look in his eyes. She was suddenly very aware of the heat of the whiskey in her stomach. Before she could think about it, before she fully understood what was happening, he was leaning toward her.

His lips were firm and warm against hers. She opened her mouth and returned the kiss, her whole body arching to meet him. He pulled her sideways onto the couch.

She twisted around to straddle him, pushing him back into the cushions. She tasted whiskey on his tongue. The moment stretched out, intense, explosive.

Then Erin was suddenly sane again, sane and stone-cold sober, still a little dizzy, but clear-headed. She pulled away from him abruptly and stood, turning away.

"Erin, darling," Carlyle began.

"I have to go," she said. She still couldn't make eye contact.

"Stay. Please."

But she was already on her way out the door, moving so fast she was almost running down the stairs. She burst into the Barley Corner's back hall, pushed past a couple of patrons outside the restroom, and made for the back door. Caleb, the guy in charge of the Corner's security, was standing there. He watched her go with a look that might have been amusement, but she hardly noticed him. She shoved open the door and hit the alley, running now. She'd walked to the Corner, since it was just a few blocks from her apartment. She ran halfway home, finally slowing to a walk when she knew she was out of sight of the place.

Rolf greeted her at the door, tail wagging. She thrust him to one side, stumbled into the bathroom, and stared at herself in the mirror, hands braced on the sink.

"Oh, God," she said. "What the hell did I do?" She looked into her own tired eyes for an answer that wasn't there. "What did I do?"

And that wasn't the real question. The real question was, what would she do next?

Here's a sneak peek from Book 6: Black Magic

Coming 2019

"Five! Four! Three!"

Erin O'Reilly braced herself. She tried to look confident. She remembered what her dad had told her.

"When you're a cop, you always need to look like you're in control. Especially when you're not."

"Two! One!"

This was it. She took a deep breath.

"Happy New Year!"

She thought she heard the roar clean down from Times Square, but that was unlikely. She was watching the ball drop on her brother's TV set in his Midtown brownstone. But cars were honking their horns outside and people were cheering, all over the city.

Erin's brother, Sean Junior, put his arms around his wife, Michelle, and gave her a kiss.

"Eww," Anna said, hiding her face in her hands. Erin's niece had only just turned eight. She wouldn't think kisses were anything but gross for a few years yet, thank God. Anna's little brother, Patrick, hadn't quite made it to midnight. He was curled up at one end of the couch, fast asleep in spite of the racket.

Erin turned to the guy she'd brought to their little New Year's party. "How about it, partner? A kiss for good luck?" She bent over and brought her face close to his.

Rolf extended his tongue and licked her chin.

"Good boy," she said and rubbed her K-9 behind the ears. She wasn't feeling very celebratory, but spending the evening with her brother and his family beat drinking at home. And she'd been doing too much of that lately.

"You could've brought a date," Michelle said. She raised her champagne glass and clinked it to Sean Junior's, then Erin's.

"Dogs are better company than boyfriends," Erin said.

"Says you," Michelle said, winking.

"Anna, back me up on this," Erin said. "Who would you rather have at a party? A boy, or Rolf?"

"Rolfie!" Anna said in tones of finality.

Erin shrugged. "I guess that's settled."

"Come on, Erin," Michelle persisted. "You can't not have a date on New Year's Eve!"

"God, Shelley. You're starting to sound like my mom."

Michelle smiled. "Are you working in a police station, or a convent?"

"What's a convent?" Anna asked.

"It's where I'll put you once the boys start sniffing around you," Sean said. "Ow!"

Michelle pretended she hadn't just shot her husband an elbow and kept looking at Erin.

"What?" Erin demanded.

Michelle raised an eyebrow and waited.

"Sis, I interrogate crooks for a living," Erin said. "I'm not gonna give you anything."

"So there is something," Michelle said triumphantly. "Okay, spill."

"No!"

"There must be a reason you don't want to tell me," Michelle said. "Let's see. Oh, I know! It's another cop. Maybe one your dad knows?"

Erin didn't want to play this game. "Think what you want," she said. "It's late, and I work in the morning. Vic's gonna be hung over, so I'll have to pick up his slack."

Michelle pouted a little. "Erin, something's been bothering you all season, and I'm guessing it's guy trouble. You were grumpy at Christmas, admit it."

"I was not!"

It was Michelle's turn to look to her family for support.

"I take the Fifth," Sean said, turning his attention to the TV.

"Fifth what?" asked Anna.

"Amendment," Erin said. "It's something people say when they're guilty but don't want to say so. And I was not grumpy!"

"Yes, you were," Anna said. "But it's okay, Aunt Erin. We love you anyway."

"She's right," Michelle said. "It's okay. But what's eating you? You don't have to tell me now. But you probably should tell somebody, sometime. The job you do, it's not good to be distracted."

Erin didn't have an answer, because Michelle was right. She was distracted, and it was guy trouble. It'd been a little over two months since she'd let her emotions get the better of her judgment. As a result, she'd gotten too close to a guy who was, to put it mildly, a risky relationship prospect. Morton Carlyle was handsome, charming, and witty. He was also a mid-level member of the Irish mob, a career criminal, and a very dangerous man to be associated with. Erin had spent the past ten weeks trying to forget their last encounter had happened, with a complete lack of success.

She was aware Michelle was still watching her with sisterly concern. It irritated her.

"I've got plenty of worse things to worry about than whatever crazy ideas you've got about my love life," she said. "You do know my job involves people who kill other people, right?"

"That's true," Michelle said. "But I'm not qualified to give you advice on that part of your life."

Erin had to bite her tongue not to ask Michelle how being a stay-at-home mom qualified her to give advice on Erin's relationship status. "I really do need to get going," she said instead, draining the last of her champagne. "Thanks for having me over."

"No problem," Sean said, turning back toward her now that the girl talk seemed to be over. "Here, I'll give you a good-luck kiss." He planted a brotherly smack on her cheek.

"Me, too." Michelle followed up on Erin's other cheek. "You should come over more, Erin. Don't be such a stranger."

"Between my hours and hers, it's a wonder she and I even know we're still alive," Sean said. He was a trauma surgeon who often worked long night shifts, and Erin was a detective with the NYPD's Major Crimes Division. "I just hope our professional lives stay as separate as possible."

"Me, too," Erin said. She got her jacket out of the hall closet. "Good night, Shelley, Sean, Anna. Hope this year is better than the last."

"Always," Sean said. "And I hope our jobs are boring and uneventful."

Erin's job stayed that way almost until she'd gotten back to her own apartment. Then her phone rang, and things got weird in a hurry.

*   *   *

"Where are you?" were the first words Lieutenant Webb said.

"South Manhattan," Erin replied.

"You sober?"

"Yeah. What's up?"

"Get to Midtown West right now. Theater District, Forty-Second Street."

"On my way." Erin's heart lurched. She was thinking of all the things that could go wrong in a crowded theater. Fire, gas leak, bomb, active shooter.

Her car was an unmarked black Charger with a special compartment for Rolf in the back. She put on the low-profile flashers and siren and sped up. In October she and her squad had barely managed to stop a terrorist from blowing up a big chunk of central Manhattan. What if they were too late this time? "I'm fifteen minutes out," she said. "What've we got?"

"One victim."

"Just one?" Erin was relieved but confused. "Why isn't a Homicide squad handling it?"

"According to the responding officer, it's a strange one," Webb said. "Apparently the victim was cut in half."

"In half?"

"That's what I said."

"We got any witnesses?"

"Apparently about six hundred."

Erin wasn't sure she'd heard right. "Six hundred?"

"O'Reilly, this will be a long conversation if you repeat everything I say."

"What happened?"

"I'd say it's our job to figure that out, being detectives and all. Sounds like an actress got cut in half on stage, in the middle of a performance."

"Jesus."

"I don't think so, but it's a little early to rule out any suspects," Webb said dryly. "We'll know more soon. I'm just about on site. Neshenko's on his way. See you in a few."

*   *   *

Broadway was packed with over forty theaters. But it wasn't hard to tell which one Erin was looking for. Half a dozen squad cars were out front, their blue-and-red flashers competing with the marquee lights. The sign over the theater proclaimed THE GREAT RONALDO'S PHANTASMAGORIA in blood-red letters. Big posters on either side of the entrance depicted a mysterious black-cloaked figure standing behind a screaming woman strapped to a table while a buzz-saw chewed through the wood. Under the circumstances, Erin found the posters in very bad taste.

She parked with the rest of the police vehicles, retrieved Rolf from the back seat, showed her gold shield to the uniformed officers at the door, and went inside.

It was the busiest crime scene she'd ever investigated. People were everywhere. Most were in evening attire, suit coats and ties for the men, dresses for the women. Even the kids, and she was sorry to see a fair number of them, had on button-down shirts and cute dresses. A lot of the kids, and more than a few adults, were crying. Others had stunned, shocked expressions on their faces and seemed to be looking straight through whatever their eyes were pointed at. Erin had seen that look before, on survivors of car accidents and shootings.

A bunch of uniforms were doing their best to keep everyone in order, but there weren't enough cops on scene. Erin's instinct was to pitch in and help out. But she was a detective, and crowd control wasn't her job. She worked her way through the lobby and into the auditorium.

Lieutenant Webb and Vic Neshenko were on the stage in front of the curtain. They were talking to a tall, thin man in a tuxedo and cape; presumably, the Great Ronaldo. The curtain had been drawn down by some quick-thinking stagehand, so the crime scene wasn't visible to the audience, but Erin could see a garish fan of blood-spatter.

She and Rolf made it down to the front rows. The crowd thinned out here, and it wasn't hard to guess why. Blood had splattered clean into the fourth row. She saw stains on the upholstery, on the floor, just about everywhere. The most disturbing thing was that several seat-backs had clean patches in the center, outlining where people had been sitting.

Erin planted her hands on the edge of the stage, being careful to avoid the bloody patch, and levered herself up. Rolf leaped and scrambled up beside her. The two of them approached the other two detectives.

"O'Reilly," Webb said. "Glad you're here. This is Ronald Whitaker, otherwise known as the Great Ronaldo."

The tall man made a slight bow and smiled wanly. He'd attempted to wipe his face clean, but little spots of blood were visible around his eyebrows and his neat little black mustache and goatee.

"What happened?" Erin asked.

"If you wouldn't mind going over it again," Webb said to the magician. "From the beginning?"

"Yes, of course," The Great Ronaldo said. "We were doing our show, everything was going great. The crowd was really engaging with us. You can feel it, when the house is with you. It's an electric kind of thing, something special. Kat had a real spark to her tonight."

"Excuse me," Erin said. "Kat?"

"My assistant," he explained. "Katarzyna the Gypsy."

"That her real name?" Vic asked. The big detective's eyes were bloodshot and he looked like he'd rather be anywhere else. Erin wondered how much he'd had to drink earlier in the evening.

"No, it's Kathy... Kathy Grimes."

"Go on," Webb said. He looked tired, too, but Webb always looked tired. Erin had never seen him without bags under his eyes.

"We were all set for one of the big numbers, the table saw," Ronaldo said. "I tied her down, we got it running, and something went wrong."

"Hold it," Vic said. "That isn't a real power saw, is it?" He jerked a thumb over his shoulder toward the curtain.

"Yes, it is," Ronaldo said. "That's part of the effect. We cut through a few things just beforehand, to prove it's a real blade. For dramatic effect."

"But you don't actually cut the girl in half," Vic observed. "Usually."

Ronaldo shook his head. "No, that's never happened before."

"We're going to need you to show us how the trick is supposed to work," Webb said.

"I can't do that."

"Why not, exactly?"

"A magician can't demonstrate his tricks to just anyone, especially a non-magician."

Webb took a deep breath and looked at the ceiling for a moment. If he was looking for patience, he didn't find it there. "Mr. Whitaker," he said, returning his gaze to the man in front of him, "this is a homicide investigation. Either we're looking at a terrible accident, or premeditated murder. The amount of trouble you're in will only increase if you don't cooperate. We're going to examine the device. Your choice is whether we do it with your permission, or without it."

Ronaldo sighed. "May I rely on your professional courtesy and discretion, Detective?"

"Absolutely," Webb said, deadpan.

"Let's have a look at this thing," Vic said.

Ready for more?

Join Steven Henry's author email list
for the latest on new releases, upcoming books and
series, behind-the-scenes details, events, and more.

Be the first to know about new releases in the Erin
O'Reilly Mysteries by signing up at
tinyurl.com/StevenHenryEmail

About the Author

Steven Henry learned how to read almost before he learned how to walk. Ever since he began reading stories, he wanted to put his own on the page. He lives a very quiet and ordinary life in Minnesota with his wife and dog.

Also by Steven Henry

Ember of Dreams
The Clarion Chronicles, Book One

When magic awakens a long-forgotten folk, a noble lady, a young apprentice, and a solitary blacksmith band together to prevent war and seek understanding between humans and elves.

Lady Kristyn Tremayne – An otherwise unremarkable young lady's open heart and inquisitive mind reveal a hidden world of magic.

Robert Blackford – A humble harp maker's apprentice dreams of being a hero.

Master Gabriel Zane – A master blacksmith's pursuit of perfection leads him to craft an enchanted sword, drawing him out of his isolation and far from his cozy home.

Lord Luthor Carnarvon – A lonely nobleman with a dark past has won the heart of Kristyn's mother, but at what cost?

Readers love *Ember of Dreams*

"The more I got to know the characters, the more I liked them. The female lead in particular is a treat to accompany on her journey from ordinary to extraordinary."

"The author's deep understanding of his protagonists' motivations and keen eye for psychological detail make Robert and his companions a likable and memorable cast."

Learn more at tinyurl.com/emberofdreams.

More great titles from Clickworks Press

www.clickworkspress.com

The Altered Wake
Megan Morgan

Amid growing unrest, a family secret and an ancient laboratory unleash long-hidden superhuman abilities. Now newly-promoted Sentinel Cameron Kardell must chase down a rogue superhuman who holds the key to the powers' origin: the greatest threat Cotarion has seen in centuries – and Cam's best friend.

"Incredible. Starts out gripping and keeps getting better."

Learn more at clickworkspress.com/sentinel1.

Hubris Towers: The Complete First Season
Ben Y. Faroe & Bill Hoard

Comedy of manners meets comedy of errors in a new series for fans of Fawlty Towers and P. G. Wodehouse.

"So funny and endearing"

"Had me laughing so hard that I had to put it down to catch my breath"

"Astoundingly, outrageously funny!"

Learn more at clickworkspress.com/hts01.

Death's Dream Kingdom
Gabriel Blanchard

A young woman of Victorian London has been transformed into a vampire. Can she survive the world of the immortal dead—or perhaps, escape it?

"The wit and humor are as Victorian as the setting... a winsomely vulnerable and tremendously crafted work of art."

"A dramatic, engaging novel which explores themes of death, love, damnation, and redemption."

Learn more at clickworkspress.com/ddk.

Share the love!

Join our microlending team at
kiva.org/team/clickworkspress.

Keep in touch!

Join the Clickworks Press email list
and get freebies, production updates, special deals,
behind-the-scenes sneak peeks, and more.

Sign up today at clickworkspress.com/join.